THE LONDON WE LOVE

Oct. 13

TOWER BRIDGE

THE LONDON WE LOVE

by

G. E. EADES, L.C.P., F.S.A.SCOT., M.R.S.T.

LECTURER IN LONDON HISTORY, CITY LITERARY INSTITUTE
FORMERLY HISTORY MASTER, THE AVENUE L.C.C. SENIOR SCHOOL
HISTORY MASTER, THE NELSON L.C.C. SECONDARY SCHOOL
Author of "LONDON : the Romance of its Development"

Coloured plates by Rowland Hilder
Black and white drawings by Donia Nachshen

EVANS BROTHERS LIMITED, LONDON

First published 1946

PREFACE

"THE preface is the part of a book that no one reads." That was what one of my boys once said, and I think that he was right; very few people ever read the preface.

But I hope that you are going to read this preface right through to the end because I want to introduce myself to you, and I want to tell you something about the book before you begin to read it. Also I want to thank several people who have helped me to make this book and I should like you to know who they are.

I am a London schoolmaster. I was born and educated in London; I have spent more than forty years teaching London boys and girls, and for the last twenty years I have been teaching grown-up people too, many of them my old scholars, about London and its story. I have been reading that story and wandering about in London studying its people and its buildings ever since I was a London schoolboy; I have come to love London and I want you to love it too.

Now do not shut the book and say, "More dry history," because history is not dry. Learning dates is, but dates are not history any more than a row of hat-pegs is the people who hang their hats on it, and in this book there are not many dates. Besides, this is not a study book. It is a book to read for pleasure. It is a story book, the true story of the greatest and most wonderful city in the world. It is your story because you are part of London. I have not told all the story here for nobody could tell it in one book. You will find many other books about London and I hope that you will read some of them when you have finished this one.

Now for the thanks. First of all I want to thank the many friends, some of them boys and girls, who read parts of the book whilst it was being written and suggested alterations that have made it more interesting. There are also the boys and girls, as well as the adult students, who used to listen to my talks and go with me on rambles: they all helped.

Then there are Miss Nachshen and Mr. Rowland Hilder the artists, whose beautiful pictures make the book so bright; my wife, who read the manuscript and the proofs, and there are the writers of other books who have given me information and ideas. Lastly, there are the people who turned the manuscript into a book: the printers, the binders and the publishers, without whose help you would never have been able to read what I have written.

G. E. E.

5

CONTENTS

COLOURED PLATES

BLACK AND WHITE ILLUSTRATIONS

PROLOGUE

O LONDON thou art great in glory, and envied for thy greatness : thy Towers, thy Temples, and thy Pinnacles stand upon thy head like borders of fine gold, thy waters like fringes of silver hang at the hems of thy garments. Thou hast in thee that make thee fairest.

Thomas Dekker

. . . . . .

I PRAY you let us satisfy our eyes
With the memorials, and the things of fame
That do adorn this City.

William Shakespeare

. . . . .

WHEN a man is tired of London he is tired of life.

Dr. Johnson

. . . . .

IT'S a wonderful place this London; a nation, not a city; with a population greater than some kingdoms, and districts as different as if they were under different governments and spoke different languages.

Benjamin Disraeli, Earl of Beaconsfield

. . . . .

HEAVEN itself wouldn't be any use to me if it wasn't something like London. No man need hanker after Heaven as long as he's got the London streets to walk in.

Joe Stokes, of Hackney
(In a Broadcast on June 20, 1943)

. . . . . .

LONDON'S always so nice and friendly.

An Evacuee girl in 1944

CHAPTER I

THE LONDONER

WHAT do we mean when we say, " I'm a Lon-doner " ? It used to be an easy question to answer, for Londoners were those who lived in the City, that square mile in the middle of modern London which is ruled over by the Lord Mayor and was surrounded by a wall ; and it was said that the true Cockney was one born within the sound of Bow Bells. But to-day very few people live in the City, and very few babies are born there. Even the Lord Mayor lives at the Mansion House only during his year of office. Hardly any of us, therefore, can call ourselves Londoners in that sense.

Then is it anyone who works in the City ? This again will not do, for many of the City workers live at Brighton or Southend and other places forty or fifty miles away, coming up to the City every day to work ; and there are many who are Freemen of the City, yet do not work there and may never have been near it. Their fathers and ancestors were hereditary Freemen, and their sons have inherited their title and can exercise their rights at any time by taking up business in the City.

To-day, however, there are many who can call them-selves Londoners although they are not Freemen of the City. They have been born hundreds of miles away and may live and work miles away from the centre of London ; for London covers a very wide area. There are, indeed, many Londons ; and I doubt if we ought to limit the term Londoner even to those who live within the County of London. We must include those who live in the large area we call Greater London. I do not think it is entirely a question of where one lives. It is rather to be decided by how one looks at life. We must reckon as Londoners all those who, having lived in London, have been caught up by its spirit and so have a certain way of looking at life.

You will remember the great evacuation of 1939–40 when thousands of us went to live in the country. Some had relatives there and went to stay with them. Most of us knew quite a lot about the country, for we had stayed there for holidays, and our parents, perhaps, had come from the country. We all thought how nice it would be to live there ; yet, after we had been away for a few weeks, many of us wanted to come back to Town. Why ? It was not because we were lonely, for those who were not living with relatives had friends and schoolmates with them. The weather was fine and we had plenty to do. Our teachers saw to that. It was not because we could not go to the cinema, for nearly all of us were in small towns where there were cinemas, or we could get to them quite easily. Yet we found something pulling us back to London. What was it ? Our country friends rather unkindly said " Fish and chips " ; but it was not that either. I asked some of the children in my own party and I think one girl came very near to the right answer when she said, " Well, sir, in the country there's nowhere to play and nothing ever happens. It doesn't seem friendly." She was right. London is a friendly place that adopts those who come to live in it without asking them a lot of questions ; and there is always something happening. Somehow one feels at the heart of things. Wherever we or our parents were born, London takes possession of us when we come there, and after a time we cannot be really happy anywhere else. We have become Londoners.

The real mark of the Londoner is not the so-called Cockney accent, or even that perky manner that so many of us seem to have—our country friends call it cheekiness. It is just that feeling of loneliness that he has when he is away from London. Joe Stokes, of Hackney, knew exactly what the spirit of London was when he said in a broadcast one summer evening in 1943 :

" Mind you, Heaven itself wouldn't be any use to me if it wasn't something like London.

" No man need hanker after Heaven as long as he's got the London streets to walk in and the people to talk to, and ' daffs ' and tulips to buy in Covent Garden Market, and a barrow to push from Covent Garden to Highbury and from Highbury along to Stamford Hill, and from Stamford Hill about six o'clock in the evening down home to Hackney."

So if, having been born anywhere in the London area, or having come to live and work there, you feel as Joe Stokes did, then you are a Londoner. You are one of that great company that includes Thomas Becket and Geoffrey Chaucer, Spencer, Ben Jonson and Milton, Samuel Pepys and Dr. Johnson, Thomas More and Charles Dickens, Richard Whittington and Thomas Gresham, and the thousands more who, although their very names are forgotten, have all given something to make the spirit of London.

GEOFFREY CHAUCER
(*After a painting in the National Gallery*)

The first Londoners of whom we know anything at all certain are those English who for over a century fought the Danes and marched out against William the Conqueror at Hastings. There were others, Romans and Roman Britons, before them; for London was founded nearly two thousand years ago. These Roman Britons had built up a great trading centre on the banks of the Thames very soon after the Romans first came to the country; and at the end of the Roman period, four hundred years later, their descendants had fought against the Saxon invaders. But, apart from a few bits of mosaic pavement, the foundations of some of their buildings, and a few odds and ends of the things they used, we have nothing to tell us what sort of people they were or how they lived.

It is not until Norman times that we begin to get anything like a clear picture of the Londoner as he really was, and by then the city was nearly a thousand years old and had been inhabited continuously all the time. Then we see the citizens marching out to Hastings to fight the invader and defend their liberties, and we meet them again a few months later, still undefeated, making a treaty with William. And that is the picture that persists through the centuries. Always the Londoner is one who values liberty so much that he is ready to fight for it.

These Saxon Londoners, like ourselves, were drawn from all over the country and from many places in Europe; for, all through her history, London has drawn her citizens from many parts. Men and women have come there from the country villages of England and Wales. There have been Scots and Irish, Germans and Frenchmen, Italians and Spaniards. They have all come to live in London and they have all become Londoners, forgetting whence they came.

Take, for example, the great Thomas Becket, Archbishop of Canterbury; St. Thomas of London to every medieval Englishman. His father, Gilbert, came from Rouen, and his mother from Caen, although according to medieval legend she was a Saracen princess from the Holy Land. Yet Thomas was a Londoner and loved his city so well that when his secretary was writing his master's life he felt it necessary to include a description of the city and its people so that his readers might understand what sort of man Thomas was. Dick Whittington, four times Lord Mayor, came up from a Gloucestershire village where his father was the squire. The ancestors of Sir Thomas More and Sir Thomas Gresham were country people. So were the parents of John Milton and Samuel Pepys ; whilst Dr. Johnson and many others of those who loved London most were themselves country people who did not come to London until they were grown up. But all alike were Londoners, full of that spirit of liberty and that love for London that is the mark of the true Londoner in all ages.

Let us try to see how these Londoners lived and worked in the past. Down to the end of the eighteenth century they all lived within the City or just outside its walls ; the merchants over their warehouses, the shopkeepers over their shops and the working people in the narrow lanes that still run down from Cheapside to the river. They were a rough lot, those early Londoners, always fighting amongst themselves ; but if anyone said anything against their city they were on to him like a swarm of angry bees.

In the Middle Ages the merchants and craftsmen were all members of the guilds. No one but a guildsman could trade or work in the city, and it was only the guild members who had any say in its government. To become a member a boy had to be apprenticed, usually for seven years from the age of fourteen, but generally he was sent by his parents to live with his future master when he was much younger. He spent his earlier years in going to school to learn reading and writing ; he learned good manners, how to wait at table and to do simple household tasks ; he escorted his mistress to church, and he made himself generally useful in the house, even minding the baby. Then, when he was about fourteen years old, the boy was taken by his parents or his master to a guild meeting and there bound apprentice for seven years. For a while longer he went to school, but he got most of his learning by working at his trade. He learned how his craft was managed, how the city was governed and what was going on in the world by going with his master to guild meetings and listening to the discussions there, by hearing the conversation when he was waiting at table, and by going on journeys, even to foreign cities : for London-made goods were in demand all over Europe.

Life, however, was not all work. Whenever there was a wedding or other festivity in the street all the apprentices left their work and joined in the fun ; and, until they had seen everything and thoroughly enjoyed themselves, no one could get them back to work. In the winter they skated on the frozen ponds in Finsbury and Moorfields, fastening the bones of animals to their shoes for

skates ; they played football and quarterstaff in the streets ; they were drilled and practised in archery after morning church on Sundays and Holydays ; they fought one another and the lads of rival guilds ; they had sports on the river ; and they set up maypoles to dance round on May Day. On Midsummer Eve they lit fires and feasted in the streets, afterwards going out into the country to spend the

SAMUEL PEPYS
(*After a painting by Amy Scheffer*)

night in the fields in the hope of seeing fairies. They took part in all the processions and pageants. The cry "Clubs, Clubs!" would bring them pouring out of the shops, ready to defend one another or their city, and, once they were roused, only the armed forces of the city could get them back to work.

It was not only the apprentices who fought ; their masters often took a hand too. Once the fishmongers and the poulterers started a fight, probably over some rude remarks shouted about the quality of the fish or poultry in rival shops. From shouting they came to pelting one another with their goods, and then they took to swords and axes and a real battle was soon in progress. The Lord Mayor called out the armed forces and in trying to restore order he was struck by some missile. Now to kill a man in a street brawl was not considered very serious; a fine paid to the City, a present to the widow and a donation to his guild for masses to be sung for his soul, was sufficient atonement; but to blacken the eye of the chief magistrate was a different matter. No fine could atone for that, and so the leading fishmongers and poulterers were hanged as a warning to others.

On another occasion there was a great football match between the men of London and those of Westminster, the field being the country between the two cities. Football in those days was a dangerous game; Edward I had forbidden it because so many players were killed. On this occasion, as the Westminster men found they were losing, they armed and drove the Londoners off the field, back to their city. There they in turn armed and made a sortie, driving off the Westminster men and killing several of them. Finally they set fire to the Abbey gateway, which was their opponents goal, and the King's knights had to come out of the Palace with their men-at-arms to drive them away.

The great event in the life of an apprentice was the day when he had finished his training and was ready to be passed as a master workman. For some months he had been busy on a piece of work which he himself had designed and which he had to make himself—his masterpiece, which was to prove his skill. At last the great day dawned. All the members of the guild went in procession from their hall to the church of their patron saint where they heard Mass. After this they went back to the hall, elected new officers and filled any vacancies in the livery. Then the young men who had finished their apprenticeship were called up to the platform where they showed their work. Their masters and other leading men of the guild testified to their ability and character, and the masterpiece of each lad was passed round for inspection. If his masterpiece were approved, the apprentice was admitted a full member of his craft. He was now free to set up for himself; he had a vote in the affairs of the guild and of the city ; if he wished, he could get married. The usual practice, however, was for the young man to work for at least a year as a journey-man in order to gain more experience. Often he would go abroad for this, carrying letters of recommendation to masters in some foreign city where he could get new ideas before he came home and set up for himself.

The guilds did a great deal more than just train apprentices. They supervised all the work done by the masters and they made rules governing the quality of the work, the hours of labour and the price at which goods were to be sold. All work had to be done in daylight and in full view of the street, so that everyone could see that it was done honestly. Inspectors were appointed to see that the rules were obeyed and offenders were very severely punished. On one occasion a fish-monger was found guilty of selling stale fish. He was made to stand in the pillory at his shop door with a neck-lace of the fish round his neck and afterwards " the said fish " were burned " under his rascally nose." A wine-merchant who watered his wine was ordered to stand in a barrel of it at his shop door and, because it was sour, he was made to drink a quart of it. The baker who gave short weight was drawn through the city with a necklace of his light loaves, loaded with lead, hanging round his neck. The master or journeyman who continued to break the rules was turned out of his guild, which meant that he had to leave London and become an outlaw, for no other place would have him ; whilst the idle or careless apprentice was whipped, first by his master and, if that had no effect, then in public by order of the guild.

There is still in existence the account of one such punishment. A boy called John Rolls was accused by

A FISHMONGER IS PILLORIED FOR SELLING BAD FISH. THE
OFFENDING FISH IS STRUNG ROUND HIS NECK

his master of careless work, and, as private whippings
failed to cure him, he was brought before the Wardens
at the next meeting of the Guild. John was tried and
found guilty. So, says the record :

> The Wardens caused to be made two porter's frocks with hoods to
> cover the face. The next Court day two tall men, having the frocks on
> them, came in with two pennyworth of birchen rods, and without
> speaking any words they pulled off the doublet and shirt of the said
> John Rolls and there upon him they spent all the rods for his unthrifty
> conduct.

The Londoners of those days were not allowed even
to dress as they liked. They had to dress in accordance
with rules made by the guilds and were severely punished
if they broke the rules. One of the duties of the wardens
was to see that these dress rules were kept, and they
seem to have found this a difficult matter, especially with
the ladies, who were always trying to wear a little more
silk or fur than was permitted.

The Ironmongers, for instance, were to dress, " in such wise that it be no dishonesty to the Company, but that they be apparalled reasonably and honest ; that is to say on Holydays, with throwts, hose, shirts, doublets, gowns and clokes with other necessaries convenient and clean, and on working days such as be honest and profitable to keep them from the cold and wet, and they shall not suffer their hair to grow long." (Long hair was only allowed to nobles, knights and gentry.)

A Merchant Taylor, quite a wealthy and important citizen, was sent to prison by order of his guild because he came to a meeting dressed as a gentleman and wearing " a cloke of pepadore, a pair of hose lined with taffety (silk stockings), and a shirt edged with silver." Shakespeare was probably thinking of these dress rules when he wrote :

> What, know you not,
> Being mechanical you ought not walk
> Without the sign of your profession.

The great merchants lived in tall houses whose upper stories projected so far out over the street that people from their upper windows could shake hands with their neighbours across the road. In the attics slept the maids ; below were the bedrooms and the living-rooms, and on the ground floor was the shop or workroom where the apprentices worked by day and slept by night. Underground were the cellars where food and goods were stored.

The ordinary citizens lived in houses of two rooms, the front one with a window opening on to the street. This was the workshop. Behind was a smaller room which was living-room and kitchen combined, and behind this a lean-to shed containing a good store of barrels for the salt meat, the flour and the ale that formed their chief food. Above, there was usually an attic bedroom reached by a ladder and containing a bed built into the wall like a cupboard with a shutter that closed it in completely. The riverside workers and the labourers lived in one-roomed huts, which they shared with the pigs and the poultry.

The furnishings of the house of an ordinary citizen are very interesting, and there are a number of wills and other records from which a very good idea of the contents of these houses can be gained. One we know contained one room, with a small kitchen and an attic bedroom. In this bedroom there was a bed, apparently a four-poster imported from Flanders, three feather beds, two pillows and a great chest in which were six woollen blankets, eight linen sheets, four tablecloths, and a coverlet with silky shields sewn on to it. Besides these things the house contained a table (probably on trestles), a great chair, some stools and benches, and a number of brass pots and pans, wooden and pewter plates, pots and tankards, and many barrels. As for clothes, there were three or four cloaks with hoods, one or two of fine Flanders cloth, a scarlet gown trimmed with fur (evidently the guild livery), and, for the housewife, one camis and six aprons. Not much for the lady ; but, then, most of her outer clothes would have been exactly the same as those worn by the men. For the man there were a great bow, a sword, an iron headpiece and a quilted pullover strengthened with steel plates sewn all over it. In addition to these things there were curtains to hang at the door and windows to keep out the draught, and a green carpet, which would be hung on the wall like a piece of tapestry, for the floors would either be sanded or covered with rushes.

The medieval citizens were very proud of their city. In spite of its narrow streets and dark houses, its noise and its smells, they thought it was the finest place on earth, and were always ready to fight for it against the king and his nobles or against any foreign country. They loved it and were proud of it. They made it famous throughout Europe.

Changes came slowly but surely. Gradually, as foreign trade increased, the merchants became more important than the craftsmen, and their great company—the Merchant Adventurers, founded in the time of Edward I to push London's trade into Germany—began in the days of Whittington to send ships out to the Mediterranean and to exchange London goods for spices from the East and the beautiful glass and other manufactures of Italy. But it was the discovery of America and the dissolution of the monasteries that brought the first great changes in the lives of the Londoners. The monks and the nuns had to find other work, and many of those who had been employed by them had to look for new jobs. As they were not guildsmen they could not be employed in any of the old crafts, and so new trades were set up— glass and papermaking, the manufacture of arms and armour, bricks and pottery, weaving in wool and silk, shipbuilding, and many other trades. All these had to be set up outside the city, for the guildsmen would not allow them to be carried on inside ; and large numbers of German, Dutch, Flemish and French workers were brought over to practise them and to teach the English workers.

Although the new workmen learned their trades by apprenticeship there was very little control, and, as most of the new trades were on a large scale and needed a good deal of money to start them and keep them going, the workers could never become masters but remained wage-earners all their lives. This meant that there was growing up outside the city a new London whose people were not freemen, who were not so interested in its welfare and who lived very different lives from those of the citizens.

Much of the old life of the city remained right through Tudor times. The noisy street games were still prac- tised—dancing round the maypole on May Day, sword and buckler fighting, cudgel play, Morris dancing, football on Shrove Tuesday and archery practice every

Sunday; but to these were added bull and bear baiting, cock fights and dog fights, games on the river and many other rough sports.

Above all, there were the stage plays, a new thing then, as new as the cinema to-day. The first theatre was opened in Curtain Road, Shoreditch, in 1570; and in less than ten years there were five playhouses, with eighteen companies of actors and with Shakespeare, Ben Jonson and many others writing plays as fast as they could. The theatres were all outside the city, for none were allowed inside. The civic authorities thought they were far too rowdy; besides, as they were all

CHARLES DICKENS
(*After a painting by Amy Scheffer*)

made of wood, there was too much danger of fire. They were round or octagonal in plan, looking from the outside something like a windmill. Inside there was an open space, the ground or pit, with a roofed stage at one side and galleries round the others. People paid a penny for admission to the pit (a penny was a lot of money in those days), more for admission to the galleries and still more for a seat at the side of the stage, where they could criticize the play and interfere with the players.

Ben Jonson tells us in one of his plays how these people behaved :

"Now, Sir, suppose I am one of your genteel auditors that am come in, having paid my money at the door, and here I take my place and sit down : I have my three sorts of tobacco in my pocket, my light by me and thus I begin : ' By this light I wonder that any man is so mad as to come to see these rascally tits here. They act like so many wrens, not a fifth part of a good face among them. And then their ditties, most lamentable things. By this light, an it were not for tobacco the very stench of them would poison me.'"

It was the gentry who sat on the stage or in the galleries; the merchants and tradesmen occupied the pit. Few workmen ever went, for they had neither the money nor the time to spare. They had taverns where they could go when the day's work was done and they had the free entertainment of the streets. On the ninth of November there was the Lord Mayor's Show, going slowly down Cheapside to Old Swan Stairs and then by river to Westminster Hall, each one of the companies trying to put on a better pageant than the others. On Midsummer Eve there was the " Marching Watch " when the streets were illuminated, great bonfires were lighted at all the corners and the Lord Mayor with the aldermen all in full armour and assisted by numbers of knights from the King's Court, led the train-bands through the chief streets in a great procession with torch-bearers, fifes and drums and many fireworks.

Then, too, there were the Royal progresses, when the Sovereign went in state through the city accompanied by the Lord Mayor, sheriffs and aldermen and greeted by pageants at all the principal stopping places. On such occasions, carpets and rich stuffs were hung from the balconies of the houses, whose windows were crowded with the wives and daughters of the citizens and the ladies of the Court, all in their finest dresses. The streets below were lined by the train-bands in their uniforms and the members of the guilds in their coloured gowns and hoods, whilst the humble citizens saw all they could from their places on the footway. Afterwards the conduits ran wine and there was feasting and dancing in the streets all night.

There was always a free show in St. Paul's Cathedral, the nave of which was a public meeting-place. Here came the fashionable young gallant to show off his new finery and the pickpocket to relieve him of his purse;

A Theatre in the Time of Queen Elizabeth

serving-men came to find new masters and tradesmen to
get customers.   The tailor came with his sketch-book to
draw the new fashions, the captain to get recruits for the
wars in Germany, or a venture to the Indies ; poets came
to recite their latest verses ; wealthy city merchants were
on the look out for a chance to get a country estate by
lending money to the owner, or to become gentlemen by
marrying their daughters to the sons of noblemen.   All
were there to provide free entertainment for the citizens.

With the coming of the Puritans much of all this
gaiety disappeared, some of it going to Westminster
where was the King's Court, some of it being put down
by the clergy and the leading citizens.   But even Cromwell's Londoners were not the sour, long-faced, psalm-
singing figures we have learned to think they were.
Dancing in the streets was forbidden, but it went on
indoors and so too did singing ; for in those days, when
everyone could sing, cooks and housemaids were often
engaged as much on account of their singing voices as
on their skill in their work.

The Plague and the Fire brought other great changes.
About half the people were killed by the Plague, and
three-quarters of the houses were destroyed by the Fire.
So the new city was a very different place from the old.
Many of the houses were never rebuilt and two sorts of
people, the great merchants who governed London, and
the poorer people who did the work, never went back ;
only the craftsmen and the tradespeople returned.   The
merchants moved out to great houses in the country
villages of Bethnal Green or Camberwell ; the workmen
crowded into the slums of Southwark or St. Giles-in-the-
Fields.   The city was now a place where thousands
worked but in which only hundreds lived.   In the houses
of the tradesmen, who still lived over their shops, there
was more and better furniture made by London craftsmen
in the beautiful fashion set by Sheraton and Chippendale,
tea and coffee were coming into use and there were lovely
muslins and cottons for the ladies to wear.   Life was

altogether more pleasant than it had ever been before.

The skilled craftsmen shared in this prosperity; but for the labourers, life was very hard. They were constantly out of work; they lived in wretched hovels in the slums and they were driven to theft and highway robbery in the effort to keep alive. Instead of the modern police there were only old watchmen who were afraid to interfere with the gangs of roughs who infested the dark streets and even attacked well-armed gentlemen in broad daylight. In the city itself some sort of order was kept, and as householders were obliged to hang out a lantern at their doors from sunset until midnight on moonless nights the streets were not quite dark. In the new suburbs of Bloomsbury and other places there were no regulations of this sort, and so travelling was difficult and the link boy with his torch was very useful.

There was a good deal more going on in the streets than there is now, although there was less traffic. Travelling workmen came round to mend chairs or pots and pans; there was the water-carrier with his wooden tubs, the milkmaid who drove her cows round to the houses of her customers, the bear-ward with his dancing bears and the organ-grinder with his monkey. On May Day the Morris dancers and Jack-in-the-Green danced through the streets with pipe and tabor; on Midsummer Day there were puppet shows, and on the Fifth of November guys were brought round, not by small boys but by men, who made effigies of unpopular politicians and afterwards burned them in some public place. Punch and Judy did their act in their travelling theatre, as they do now; there were ballad singers with their songs and all sorts of people with things to sell. All of these had their own singing cries, each set to its own special tune like that used by the lavender seller.

Who'll buy___ my sweet la-ven-der___

All have gone now, driven away by modern traffic, though we still have the street traders with their barrows.

Londoners of the eighteenth century, even if well-to-do, spent very little time in travelling and had few holidays. A Sunday stroll in the Royal Parks or in the fields about Islington or Camberwell, a half-day at Hampstead or on Blackheath was as much as they could manage. For such an outing very careful preparations had to be made ; for, as John Gilpin found, it was a risky business and almost anything might happen. Some of the wealthy citizens did manage a week at Bath or Tunbridge Wells, but even they spent most of the year in London or at their country houses in Dulwich or Streatham. For amusements they went to the theatre or had an evening at Vauxhall Gardens, where they could enjoy music and dancing in company with others of their own class.

During this century very many people came to London from the country or from Europe. Every year hundreds of young people, like Dr. Johnson and his friend David Garrick, came up to London in the hope of making their fortunes ; and whenever there was war in Europe or some upheaval such as the French Revolution, thousands came to Britain and many of them settled in London where they introduced new industries.

The rebuilding after the Fire had brought many carpenters and builders; the desire for better furniture brought cabinet makers and upholsterers; French silk weavers came to Spitalfields and porcelain workers to Bow, Battersea and Chelsea. Shipbuilding was carried on at Deptford and Limehouse and, towards the end of the century, engineering works were set up in Southwark. All these trades brought new people into the London area, but unfortunately they never really became Londoners in the way that the earlier inhabitants had been. In those earlier days the country gentry had sent their sons to be apprenticed in the city where they worked side by side with the merchants and craftsmen's sons and became citizens.

But in the eighteenth century trade was no longer thought to be respectable for gentlemen's sons, and so the leading positions in the city fell into the hands of men of quite humble origin whose only claim to distinction was their money. They were despised by the gentry and in their turn they looked down on the craftsmen from whose class they had come and who were rapidly becoming mere wage-earners. Class distinctions became very marked, and the city was lost in the Greater London that was growing up around it, a London without unity whose people had little interest in its well-being.

The Londoner was slowly changing; yet, in spite of all changes, he remained much the same. As more and more houses were built Londoners began to sort themselves out, each kind living in a different part. Districts could then be distinguished by the kind of people who lived in them. Along the river, in the East End and in the manufacturing districts like Battersea or Wandsworth, were the artisans and labourers, the typical Cockneys with their shrill speech, their quick ways and their humour. By the middle of the nineteenth century there were dense masses of them in the inner areas, living near their work because they could not afford the time or the money for travelling. They had few amusements and worked very long hours, there were no football matches for them to watch on Saturday afternoons, no cinemas, no wireless in their homes and none of the opportunities for cheap travel that we enjoy to-day. Even if they could read, books were too expensive for them to buy, and there was very little for them to do except sit in the public-house and drink, or, if they were too respectable for this, to join a political club or a society at some church or chapel. The children and young people had only the streets in which to play and as these were badly lighted they were very unsafe for people from the more respectable parts.

Farther out, in Camberwell or Streatham, lived the clerks, the shop-workers and the civil servants, men (for until the end of the nineteenth century women went only into domestic service or factories) who could afford to travel to their work and had perhaps a week's holiday in the year which they spent at Brighton or Margate. These people lived in comfortable houses, each with its own garden; they sent their children to day grammar schools or to private schools; they had a piano in the parlour which their daughters learned to play; they went to the theatre occasionally; they attended church or chapel on Sundays, read the papers and, as young men, often joined some literary society where they discussed books or politics. The children had parks in which to walk, but there were very few games, for football and cricket did not become common until the 'nineties, and lawn tennis was played only by those who had a garden large enough for a court.

Farther out still, at Blackheath, Sydenham or Hampstead, the wealthy business men lived, with the lawyers and other professional men from the Bloomsbury squares. Those who lived in the suburbs had large houses with big gardens; they had their own carriages, kept a big staff of servants, sent their sons to boarding-schools and had governesses for their daughters. They gave dinner-parties and dances occasionally, went away to the seaside for a month each year and to the theatre or a concert during the winter. But they, like the artisans and the clerks, took little interest in London, and it began to look as though the real Londoner would soon die out and his place be taken by someone who merely worked in London but whose interests lay outside.

After about 1890 things began to improve. The population was increasing and large numbers still came up from the country; even thirty years ago more than half of the people of London had been born in country villages. But trams and buses made it easier to get about; hours of work became shorter; there were more holidays and more amusements. The bicycle made it easier for thousands of young people to get out into the country on summer evenings and for week-ends ; later on the motor-car made it easier still for people to travel. More games pitches were laid out in the parks and lawn tennis became popular. Then the cinema made entertainment cheap enough for everyone; people went out more and mixed together as they had done in earlier days. The scattered, isolated groups began to draw together and to discover that they all belonged to one society.

So the people of London began to discover that, whether they lived in Streatham or Poplar, Greenwich or Hammersmith they were all members of one great society, that they were all Londoners with many interests in common and many problems which they would have to tackle together. Thus we come to ourselves, the citizens of London to-day.

We have inherited the great traditions of our ancestors, the Londoners who lived in the city in earlier centuries. We have a bigger London, but many of its problems are the same as theirs and we shall have to solve them by working together as they did, building up for our greater London as fine a tradition as they did for their much smaller city, and handing down to our descendants as fair an heritage as we have received.

CHAPTER II

LONDON THROUGH THE AGES

HOW did London begin? John Stow, the tailor who was its first historian, tells us that after the Greeks had taken Troy by means of their wooden horse, one of the Trojan princes, Brutus, the son of Aeneas who is said to have founded Rome, sailed away westward through the Mediterranean Sea, passed the Pillars of Hercules, and, after crossing the Bay of Biscay and sailing up the English Channel, came at last to the white cliffs of a country which he called Albion. Here he turned north, and entering a wide estuary (that of the Thames) sailed up the river until he came to a place where there were some low hills. He landed, and after a fierce battle with the natives, who were led by a giant, Gogmagog, whom Brutus fought and killed, he built a city on the highest hill. This city was at first called Troynovant, that is New Troy, but was later renamed London or Lud's Town after King Lud, the son of Brutus.

That story is only a legend, but it is a very old legend, for it is told by Geoffrey of Monmouth in the early Middle Ages, and he found it in the works of an historian who was writing at the time of the English conquest. The legend was believed by centuries of Londoners and in the Guildhall there were two wooden figures of giants called Gog and Magog. These figures used to be carried every year in the Lord Mayor's Show and as one was dressed in Roman costume whilst the other was dressed as a wild man, they were evidently intended to represent Brutus and the native leader whom he defeated. There is also Ludgate Hill with St. Paul's Cathedral on its summit ; and, underneath the Cathedral, Sir Christopher Wren found a Roman altar to Diana with a still more ancient place of sacrifice below that.

ST. PAUL'S CATHEDRAL

There too we have Billingsgate, the oldest port of London, with a Celtic name that is probably older than Roman times. So, although we cannot say how much of truth, if any at all, there is in the legend of Brutus and his Trojans, we can certainly trace the beginnings of some sort of settlement on the Thames near this spot to the

c

days before the Romans came.   In those days the river
flowed through a great marsh and people could only live
on the low hills and the few sand-banks that rose above
the level of the floods.   On these hills the city of London
stands and the sand patches in the marsh became first,
the villages that surrounded the city, and then our
present metropolitan boroughs.

Before you begin to read about modern London you
ought to know something of its past history, because
without this knowledge the story of the people and their
buildings has no meaning.   It would be like the beads of
a broken necklace or a jigsaw of which the key is missing.
History is the string that holds the beads together and
makes them into a beautiful necklace or the key picture
that helps us fit together the odd pieces of the puzzle.

The first London that we know anything about is
Londinium, Roman London, and we do not even know
when that began.   There may have been some kind of
settlement before the Romans came, but if there were it
cannot have been of very great importance or Julius
Caesar would have mentioned it.   It cannot have been
of much importance a century later when the Claudian
invasion took place.   In that campaign there was a
battle fought somewhere on the south side of the river ;
the Britons were defeated and the Romans followed them
across the river and burned their village.   Unfortunately
the Roman historian who tells the story of the conquest
has not told us where the battle was fought; it might
have been anywhere along the river from Southwark
up to Richmond.   Had the village been on the site
of London some remains would probably have been
found just as the remains of the town of Cassivillunus
have been found near St. Albans or those of the headquarters of Cymbeline just outside Colchester.   But it
does not mean that there was no settlement because no
remains have yet been found ;   it may only mean that so
much digging and rebuilding has been done that all traces
of that first city have been destroyed.   All we know for

certain is that the name London is of Celtic origin and that it was a populous place in A.D. 60, only a few years after the landing of the legions of Claudius. It was in that year that Boudicca (often known as Boadicea) rebelled and her tribesmen then found that London was full of foreign merchants and, as we are told by the Roman historian Tacitus, was doing much trade. Boudicca burned the town, and its ashes have been found under Cannon Street Station, proving that Tacitus was telling the truth. He tells us too that it was so important that the Romans rebuilt it as soon as the British were defeated.

As this early Roman London was so important it must have been founded either before the legions came or very soon afterwards. Probably there was some sort of native village on Ludgate Hill with a settlement of Belgic traders at the mouth of the Walbrook, just as is found in West Africa or New Guinea to-day, and it was this settlement that the Britons destroyed in the Boudiccan revolt.

The history of London really begins with the town the Romans built after the destruction of this first settlement, for it was this town that became the city of London. From the first it was a good deal bigger than the original village, for the Romans surrounded it with a wall that enclosed the city right down to the middle of the eighteenth century, and the foundations of this wall still surround the city underground. Perhaps the best place to see the wall is at the G.P.O. in King Edward Street. Here there is a very interesting fragment with a corner bastion and, as it has been broken through at some time, it is possible to stand inside the Roman city and then to go through the wall and look at it from the outside. There is also a long piece forming the wall of cellars under some warehouses in Trinity Square, near the Tower, and a corner stands up in the grounds of the Tower itself. It is possible to walk right round London on the site of the wall. One starts from Thames Street, near St. Paul's railway station, where there was a corner of the wall. From there it went north along Water Lane, and crossed Ludgate Hill just below St. Martin's Church. Then it went on to Newgate, where it turned east to Aldersgate, and then north to a corner that can still be seen in the Rectory garden at St. Giles, Cripplegate. From here one may walk along the top of the wall—the street is called London Wall—to Bishopsgate and then by Bevis Marks to Aldgate. Here the wall turns south along the line of the Minories to the Tower. Along Thames Street there was a quay wall with ports at Billingsgate, Queenhithe, and the mouth of the Walbrook.

The new London that grew up inside the circuit of the wall was a beautiful city, with wide, straight roads, temples and public buildings, baths, shops and private houses. It had a great central forum or market-place where Leadenhall Market now stands, with a town hall on the site of the churches of St. Peter and St. Michael, Cornhill, and it was adorned with many beautiful statues. It was connected with the rest of the country by the Roman roads, all of which converged upon it ; and it must have been an important place, for the Romans gave it the title Augusta. Its streets and the foundations of its houses, the beautiful mosaic pavements of some of the buildings, the things used by its people, and even their jewels and shoes have been found and may be seen in our museums. But we know very little of its history. Only twice does anything seem to have happened. Towards the end of the third century London became the centre of the revolt of a Roman officer who called himself Emperor of Britain, and in the middle of the fourth century it was attacked and partly destroyed by a horde of Picts, Scots and English pirates, who swept through the country and finally got to London. They were driven out and the city walls repaired with the remains of the buildings they had destroyed.

Nobody knows exactly what happened to London when the real Saxon invasion began in the fifth century, but we are told in the Anglo-Saxon Chronicle that the Londoners were defeated in a battle at Crayford in the year 457 and retreated to their city, which they seem to have defended with some success for there is no record of its capture. It was not until a century later that we find any signs of the Saxons living in the city. Some writers tell us that the wars of King Arthur were fought in its defence, and that the sites of his great battles were found in the surrounding country.

Because there is no record of London in the history of the two centuries of the English conquest we must not suppose that it was deserted and in ruins. The English did not like living in towns; they preferred settlements in the country, and their villages are to be found all around London and up to within about a mile of its walls; but that does not mean that London was deserted. It may have had people living in it, descendants of the Roman Londoners and traders from the Continent and it was certainly inhabited again soon after St. Augustine came to Kent, for he sent Mellitus, one of his companions, there as bishop. From then onwards its story is continuous.

The Saxon town grew in importance right through the English period. It was once more a great trading centre with many merchants from Gaul and the Rhineland living there and when the Danes came London was strong enough to defend itself against them. Sometimes they broke in and plundered; more often they were kept out; and sometimes the Londoners sailed down the river and drove them away before they came near the city. One of these fights must have been a very exciting affair. The Danes had taken the bridge, and an army of Londoners, helped by Edmund Ironside and Olaf the Norseman, came up the river to attack them. The Danes drove off an attack on the bridge from the Southwark side, and so the attackers tried a stratagem. They strengthened their ships and covered them with raw hides so that they should not be set on fire. Then they

rowed up stream just as the tide was turning, fastened
the ships to the piers of the wooden bridge and rowed
away. Helped by the tide and by the great weight of
men on the bridge they succeeded in pulling down the
whole structure and its defenders were drowned. So
famous was this destruction of the bridge that songs
were made about it, and I can still remember one that the
children used to sing when I was a boy. Here is the tune
and some of the words.

London Bridge is broken down,
Broken down, broken down,
London bridge is broken down,
My fair lady.

The song went on to suggest rebuilding the bridge with
sticks and straw and various other materials until it came
to a final triumphal end with—

Build it up with stone so strong,
Stone so strong, stone so strong,
Build it up with stone so strong,
My fair lady.

How it was actually rebuilt in stone and some of the
other songs that were made about it, you will read in
another chapter.

The next important happening was the Norman
Conquest. When William landed near Hastings and
King Harold came rushing down from Northumbria to
meet him, the Londoners, under their leader Ansgar,
joined the King and went with him to Senlac. Here they
fought with great bravery and when Harold was killed
and the battle lost, they retreated in good order through

the forest of the Weald and got back to their city.   Here
William found them when he appeared about a fortnight
later.   The city was too strong to be taken by storm and
William could not settle down to a siege with the winter
coming on ; so he left it, marched up the river to Walling-
ford and then round to Berkhampstead, where he was
across London's communications with the Midland
Earls.   Here he waited ; but when the Londoners saw
that the Earls had no intention of fighting they made
peace with William, electing him King of the English in
return for his promise to leave London a free city.   The
treaty made between the citizens and the King may still
be seen in the Guildhall records.   It reads :

> William the King greets William the Bishop and Godfrey the
> Portreeve and all the citizens of London, French and English, friendly.
> And I give you to know that ye be all law-worthy, as ye were in King
> Edward's day.   And I will that every child shall be his father's heir
> after his father's day and I will not suffer any man to do you wrong.
> God keep you.

The original is written in English, not in French or in
Latin as it would have been had it been drawn up by
one of William's clerks ; so it was probably drawn up
by the Londoners themselves and written down by one
of their clerks.

William knew the danger of having such a powerful,
independent city in his land, and so he built a strong castle,
the Tower of London, on the river bank just outside the
eastern wall where it could stop the citizens' trade if they
became dangerous ; and at times this fortress gave the
kings a great deal of power.   But in the end London
became far too strong for the royal fortress, and the
Tower ceased to be a danger.   This is almost the last
of the old city, for in 1087 a fire destroyed a great part
of the houses, which were probably built of wood, as
they were to be for many years to come.   The cathedral
and the churches were rebuilt in stone after the new
Norman manner, and so were some of the larger houses ;

THE TOWER OF LONDON

but most of the people continued to live in wooden houses and the city was nearly destroyed several times by fire.

Under Rufus, London suffered a great deal; but Henry I was glad to buy its support with another charter which set the city in a special place amongst the groups of barons who really made up the England of those days, and the citizens were allowed to appoint their own sheriffs and those for the County of Middlesex. This made them free to be tried in their own courts and under their own law instead of in the King's courts. From now on the city was to play a most important part in the history of the country, gradually gaining freedom for itself and helping the country to gain freedom too; for most of the liberties of Englishmen were won first by the city of London and afterwards extended to the whole country.

In the reign of Richard Lionheart there was a struggle for power going on within the city itself between the great merchants who then governed it and the craftsmen, who were organizing themselves in guilds and demanding a share in its government. This struggle went on for a long time and in the end neither side won; but in the reign of John the citizens were allowed to elect their own Mayor and in this election the craftsmen had a share. Another result was Magna Carta, that famous document upon which the liberties of all English-speaking people are based. The charter was suggested by the leaders of the Londoners and the barons at a great meeting held in St. Paul's Cathedral. A rough draft was drawn up and discussed at this meeting and it was agreed that the King should be compelled, by force if necessary, to sanction it. When the barons met the King at Runnymede the Londoners went with them and the King was forced to agree. A committee of twenty-four was appointed to see that the King kept his word and on this committee sat the Mayor and two other citizens. When John died, it was the Londoners who secured the throne for his infant son Henry.

Thomas Becket had been one of the great Londoners of this time and it was his secretary, Fitzstephen, who wrote the first description of the city that we have. It was, he said, a very beautiful place, healthy and full of gardens. There were no fewer than one hundred and forty-seven churches besides the cathedral, and many monasteries and schools. There were many restaurants too where visitors or citizens could get plenty of all the best sorts of food. Its people were brave and warlike and very fond of sports and games, whilst its merchants were wealthy, trading with all Europe.

During the next century the citizens were growing more and more powerful. Up to this time the leaders had been great merchants, men from abroad like the Boccarelli of Florence who gave their name to Bucklersbury, the Lombards who lived in Lombard Street, the Basings and the Faryngdons after whom Basinghall Street and Faringdon Street are named; but now the craftsmen were becoming important and were claiming a share in city government. By banding together into guilds they were able to get control of the city and to elect the mayor, aldermen and other important officials. The oldest of the guilds was the Weavers'; but the most powerful was that of the Mercers, still the first in importance of the great city companies. One of the earliest of the mayors was Serlo le Mercer, and during the thirteenth century there were many others whose names show them to have been craftsmen. The first mayor, however, was Henry Fitzalwyn whose name seems to show that he was a merchant and probably a Norman.

The citizen army too became very important, especially during the French Wars where the London men and ships did good service. Then, as now, the Cockneys were noted for their cheerfulness in difficult situations, for the jokes they made, and for their bravery in battle. They held the post of greatest danger in the battle of Crécy and it was largely owing to them that the battle was won by the English. In return they were given the town of Calais after its capture. The French inhabitants were turned out and Londoners put in their places, and so right up to the time of its recapture in the reign of Mary Tudor the Londoners always looked on Calais as part of their own city.

By the end of the fourteenth century the ordinary workmen and labourers were trying to get a share in the government of the city. It was they who supported the Kentishmen at the time of the Peasants' Revolt, and helped them to get possession of London and to hold it for three days. The upper class citizens, with their better arms and leadership, proved too strong for them and when Wat Tyler was killed the movement collapsed.

Then a struggle broke out between the Craft Guilds, whose members wanted cheap food and cheap raw materials imported from abroad, and the food guilds, such as the Grocers', who were opposed to the import of cheap food. The government of the city fell into the hands of a new group, the Merchant Adventurers, who were trying to build up an overseas trade, and were sending their ships into the Mediterranean, taking out London-made goods and bringing back the spices and Italian wares that used to be imported by the Venetians and the Genoese. One of the most important of these Adventurers was Richard Whittington (the Dick Whittington of the fairy tale) who made a great fortune out of the Mediterranean trade.

SIR THOMAS GRESHAM

(After a painting, by an unknown artist, in the National Portrait Gallery)

During the next century, when America and the sea route to India and the Far East had been discovered, these Adventurers made London one of the most important places in the world. They spent a great deal of their money in fitting out expeditions to discover new openings for trade and in extending our trade with other lands, not only in Europe but in the newly discovered parts of the world. Later they were to use their wealth and experience in founding the English Colonies in North America, and so the United States of America owes its beginnings to these London merchants.

Among the most important of the Merchant Adventurers was the Gresham family, of which the most famous member was Sir Thomas, the founder of the Royal Exchange, which he built at his own cost so that the merchants of London might have somewhere to meet instead of having to transact their business in the streets. Like Whittington, the Greshams had been countrymen, coming from the village of Gresham in Norfolk, where their ancestors were squires. Sir Thomas himself had been apprenticed to commerce, and gained his earliest experience in the office of the Merchant Adventurers at Antwerp. He was then given the task of raising loans for the English government from the German financiers. He found this a very difficult task, for the extravagance of Cardinal Wolsey had completely destroyed English credit, and the German bankers would only lend small sums at very high rates of interest and even then they insisted that part of the loan should be taken in German manufactured goods. Gresham made a complete change in policy. Instead of going to the great German bankers he persuaded the London merchants to take up the loans and at much lower rates of interest, because the money would be spent in England, so making both London and the country more prosperous and getting the Government out of the hands of the Continental moneylenders. Mary Tudor went back to the practice of borrowing abroad, but when Elizabeth became Queen she once more made Sir Thomas her agent and he very soon restored English credit. The advice that he gave to the Queen when she came to the throne of a bankrupt country is well worth studying, especially now that we have to pay for two expensive wars. I will give it in his own words and leave you to put it into modern English for yourselves :

" An it please Your Highness to restore this realm to such a state as heretofore, Your Highness hath none other way but,—

First,   When time and opportunity serveth to bring your base money into fine.

Second, Not to restore the Steelyard (the German merchants) to their usurped privileges.

Third,   To grant as few licences (monopolies) as you can.

Fourth, To borrow as little money overseas as you can.

Fifth,   To keep your credit, especially with your own merchants."

Gresham's advice was taken by the Queen; and, as a result, England was not only able to defeat the Armada but to become the most prosperous country in Europe.

We have already seen some of the changes brought about in London by the dissolution of the monasteries. The discovery of America and of the sea-route to India was even more important. A good deal of the gold and silver that the Spaniards brought from America found its way to London either as plunder from captured Spanish ships, or by way of trade with the Low Countries. This wealth made the Londoners want to get an even greater share of the trade, and so they sent out a number of expeditions to try to discover new routes to the Far East whence the bulk of the wealth was thought to come. The Cabots had sailed from Bristol, financed by the great Merchant Adventurers of that city, but most of the later expeditions were sent out by the London Adventurers and they sailed in London ships, manned by London seamen. Frobisher, Davis, Baffin and Hudson (this last a Dutchman), whose names are sprinkled all over the seas to the north of North America, all set out from London, as did Challoner and Jenkins who opened up the White Sea route to Russia. Even Drake may be considered as a Londoner to some extent for he was a barrister of the Middle Temple and his ship, *The Golden Hind*, was brought to the Thames where she lay off Deptford for many years.

The history of the next half century is the story of the struggle between the Stuart Kings and their Parliaments, which was really a struggle between the Government and London. During the early years of the century the Londoners were very busy extending their trade. They founded the Russia Company, the Turkey and the Royal Africa Companies and finally the East India Company. They used the money they gained from all this trade to finance the plantation of Ulster and the founding of the colonies along the coast of North America. It was a London merchant, John Bates, who first refused to pay illegally increased custom duties, and it was the London members of Parliament, led by John Pym, the Treasurer of the Massachusetts Bay Company, who organized the opposition to Charles I in the House of Commons. When the five members fled from the House they took refuge in the city and Charles was not strong enough to get them out. When the Civil War broke out, London provided Parliament with most of the money it needed.

Its own army, under the command of Major-General Skippon who had trained the men, fought bravely at Edgehill and repulsed Rupert's cavalry at Brentford, so

JOHN MILTON, AGED 62
(*After an engraving by William Faithorne*)

preventing the King from winning the war in the first campaign. Even after Cromwell had formed the Ironsides the Londoners still provided the bulk of the infantry for the New Model Army. They marched to the relief of Gloucester, beat the Royalists at Newbury, and, after the final defeat of the King's armies, it was the London men who besieged most of the castles and great houses in which the Royalist leaders tried to hold out. And whilst they were doing all this they produced John Milton, one of the world's greatest poets.

But the really important events in the history of London are the Plague and the Great Fire, for they destroyed medieval London. The plague year of 1665 was a dreadful time, the worst as well as the last of many plague years in London. Most of the houses were shut up and marked with a red cross to show that the inmates were suffering from the infection; the grass grew in the streets; and the only sound was that of the bell rung by the men who went round with carts to collect the dead, whom they buried in great pits outside the city. To make matters worse we were at war with the Dutch, whose fleet sailed up the Thames and burned the English ships off Chatham. Afraid as they were, however, the Londoners stayed in their city and tried to carry on with their trade as well as they could. Mr. Pepys and his clerks at the

Navy Office on Tower Hill stayed on too, doing their best to get a fleet ready for sea to fight the Dutch.

Hardly had the Plague died down than the Fire began. It started in a baker's shop at the bottom of Pudding Lane, where the Monument stands now, and it burned for nearly a week, destroying two-thirds of the houses in the city, the cathedral, most of the churches, the roof of the Guildhall, and nearly all the halls of the guilds. This was in September, 1666, but six months later, when Mr. Evelyn was inspecting the ruins, he found the pavements were so hot that the soles of his shoes were burned. The old wooden houses, heavy with paint and tar and with their cellars filled with combustibles, burned so fiercely that nothing could be done to stop the fire from spreading until some sailors, brought up from Deptford Dockyard by Mr. Pepys, suggested making a gap in front of the flames by blowing up houses. When this suggestion was reported to King Charles, who, in his shirt-sleeves and as black as a sweep, was helping people remove their furniture, he at once ordered that it should be done, and the fire was stopped. We have had our own Great Fire, when the city was set alight by the Germans, but we did have a good fire brigade that was able to prevent the fire from spreading. In 1666, they had nothing but a few leather buckets, and so they lost everything.

Many plans were made for rebuilding the city, one of the best by Sir Christopher Wren ; but planning takes time and a great business city cannot wait whilst planning committees argue with one another. So, whilst the planners talked, the citizens rebuilt their houses on the old sites, leaving Wren to rebuild the churches and the cathedral, and Edward Jarman, the City Surveyor, the halls of the companies, the Royal Exchange and other public buildings. Instead of laying out the new city on a fine plan, with wide, straight streets, it was rebuilt on the old frontages with the same narrow streets and winding lanes, with its cathedral, churches and public buildings lost behind a crowd of shops and houses. But

Wren's new cathedral and his city churches were fine buildings, beautifully proportioned inside with much finely carved woodwork, and their towers and spires were amongst the finest in the world. So far as he could Wren made London a beautiful city. The new houses were built of brick with straight fronts so that the streets looked wider and there was more air. The new sash windows too gave better ventilation in the houses. The Monument says that the city was rebuilt in three years, but this is quite wrong, for the surveyors were not appointed until March, 1667, no church was begun until 1670, and for ten years the city was largely a mass of charred ruins overgrown with weeds.

One great change made by the Fire was that a very large number of people never went back to live in the city. Only 9,000 houses were built to replace the 13,000 destroyed and many of the churches too were not replaced as the smaller population did not need them. Whole classes disappeared completely. The poorer people remained in Whitechapel, St. Giles-in-the-Fields and other districts outside the city and the great merchants moved out to country houses in Bethnal Green, Streatham and Camberwell ; only the shopkeepers and the smaller business men were left.

The destruction caused by the Fire had been so serious that the Corporation did at last make some new regulations intended to prevent such a serious outbreak occuring again. The regulations are rather amusing reading to-day, but they were meant to be taken seriously.

The city was divided into four quarters and in each there

shall be furnished and provided eight hundred leathern buckets, fifty ladders, viz., ten forty-two foot long, ten thirty foot long, ten twenty foot long, ten sixteen foot long, and ten twelve foot long ; also so many hand squirts of brass as will furnish two for each parish, four and twenty pickaxe sledges, four and twenty shod shovels.

Besides these fire-fighting appliances the companies were to provide ladders and other appliances, whilst all

LONDON FROM HAMPSTEAD HEATH

the important inhabitants were to have hand-squirts and leathern water-buckets at their houses always ready for use.   It was also ordered that on the cry of " Fire ! " every householder should station an armed man at his door to act as a fireguard, should hang out a light and put out a bucket of water.

The carpenters, masons, bricklayers and others who worked in the building trades were to form demolition parties to be at the orders of the Lord Mayor whenever there was a fire ; the porters were to mobilize in order to help people save their goods, and all other people were to keep indoors so as to leave the streets free for the fire-fighters.

During the eighteenth century, the population of the city decreased, but that of the surrounding districts increased and there was a great deal of new building especially in the East End where new factories were being built, and in Bloomsbury where the squares were being laid out, one of the finest examples of good planning to be seen anywhere in the world.   In Westminster and in Kensington too there were many new houses being built for the courtiers, the government officials and the increasing numbers of civil servants.

The story of the city itself is now almost entirely a story of commercial development.   The Bank of England was founded in the reign of William III ; during the first half of the eighteenth century the Stock Exchange was started in order to control the dealers in stocks and shares and so prevent any repetition of the South Sea Bubble ; many banks were founded ; Lloyd's Register and many other great Insurance Companies were set up and the great produce markets of Mincing Lane came into existence, so that by the end of the Napoleonic Wars London had become the commercial and financial capital of the world, a position it still holds in spite of many attempts to depose it.

The most interesting part of the story of the eighteenth century is the history of the great struggle for liberty

D

that began soon after the close of the Seven Years' War and continued right into the next century. The story of the revolt of the American Colonies is only one part of it, and in a later chapter we shall read of that struggle and of the part that London played in it. Here let us look at London's own struggle.

Up to the beginning of the quarrel with the Americans, debates in Parliament had all been held in secret although the newspapers did sometimes print what was said to be a summary of the speeches. But no reporters were present and no record of the speeches or of the proceedings was ever made public, so that the people never really knew what their M.P.s said or how they voted. So much excitement was caused by the American outbreak and so many people wanted to understand what it was all about that it was felt the public should know exactly what Parliament was doing about it all. Real newspapers too had now come into existence and their editors began to send people to the House to take down the speeches so that fairly accurate reports could be printed. Many members claimed that the editors had no right to do this and the House of Commons ordered that the printers should be arrested. As the newspapers were published in London, the printers were brought before the Lord Mayor, who released them because the Commons had ordered their arrest without getting a warrant from a city magistrate. Lord Mayor Crosby and one of the aldermen, who were members of Parliament, were then sent to the Tower by order of the Speaker and kept there until the end of the Session, when the Speaker's authority ceased and they were released. The city blazed with anger. The prisoners were visited by all the leading citizens, and when they were released the city went wild with excitement. When Parliament met again for the new Session the reporters were there and the speeches were printed, but this time the House took no notice. The matter has never been definitely settled. Speeches and reports of debates and

divisions are regularly printed by the newspapers who
send specially trained shorthand writers to take down
the debates ; there is even a special gallery set apart for
them, but any member can have them sent out by calling
the Speaker's attention to their presence, and occasionally a secret session is held when no report of the speeches
is published. There is now a report (Hansard) published
of all speeches made in every ordinary session and this is
regarded as official. So the city had won the first round
in the fight for the freedom of the Press and it is now
recognized that newspapers have the right to report
members' speeches and even to make comments on them ;
whilst the policy of the Government is regularly criticized
and often condemned.

London also took the side of Mr. Wilkes in his struggle
against " general warrants," that is warrants issued for
the arrest of a person without giving any name or specify-
ing any charge, and this struggle too was won after a long
fight, in the course of which Wilkes himself was sent to
prison. The citizens marked their appreciation of his
struggle by electing him an alderman and afterwards
Lord Mayor. Thus, by the end of the century, London
had won for the British citizen the right to know what
was going on in Parliament and to criticize not only
members but also the Government, and in addition the
right of freedom from arrest except on a warrant granted
by a magistrate and naming not only the person to be
arrested but also the charge. These two rights give to us
a great deal more freedom than is possessed by the people
of most countries outside the British Commonwealth.

The changes that were begun in the eighteenth century
continued during the nineteenth ; London became larger
and larger, whilst the city itself became more and more
a place where people worked but did not live. The most
important events in its history are the setting up of new
forms of government, and these we shall study in another
chapter. Outside the city the riverside area became
industrial and the outer areas residential, and the history

of London becomes a part of the history of the country. It still, however, took the lead in every great movement, not so much through the official action of the Mayor and Corporation as by the power of the Press. London was so big that its public opinion had become very powerful, yet it was so compact that great meetings could easily be organized and even Parliament swayed by them. So it is to the great London newspapers and to public meetings that we look for the control of public opinion during the nineteenth century, rather than to the action of the Lord Mayor and the aldermen of the city.

The City Corporation is still a great power and the Lord Mayor is one of the most important men in the world, so that people all over the world look to him for a lead in all important crises. If there is a famine, a great fire, an earthquake or any other disaster in any part of the world, the Lord Mayor is expected to open a Mansion House Fund for the sufferers ; what he says is listened to with respect in all parts of the world.

London in the nineteenth century became what Rome had been in the days of the Roman Empire, the capital of the world.

CHAPTER III

HOW LONDON GREW

IN the first chapter we found that it was very difficult
to decide who were Londoners. Now we are going
to find that it is even more difficult to say exactly what
London is, for there are so many Londons. Down to
the time of the Great Fire there was no difficulty at all.
London meant the City, the square mile ruled over by the
Lord Mayor and still enclosed by its wall ; although even
then there were people who had begun to talk of a
different London—the Town—that stretched west from
Ludgate Circus to St. James's, and included Lincoln's
Inn Fields, Drury Lane and Soho, the part where the
courtiers and the members of Parliament lived. In
the eighteenth century Bloomsbury and a big area on the
Southwark side had to be added and in the nineteenth
century the houses spread until they had covered the
whole area from Hammersmith in the west to the River
Lea in the east and from the Crystal Palace in the south
to Hampstead Heath in the north.

By this time people had begun to see that the whole
of this district must have some sort of central control,
because it was really all one although there were many
governing bodies. There was great confusion about such
things as drains and main roads, and so a new body was set
up to control these and a new name was found for this
district ; it was called the Metropolis. But before that
an even larger area had been marked out, the Metropolitan
Police District ; and there were to be more Londons
before the end of the century. The City of London is
just about one square mile in area ; Police London is about
700 square miles ; and some of the others are even
larger. Down to 1905 there was a School Board London,
and after 1898 the County of London, each covering the
same district, an area of about 100 square miles. Since

the beginning of the present century other Londons have been set up. There is the Port of London, extending along the river from Teddington to the Nore; Water London, the great district supplied by the Metropolitan Water Board; Postal London of 230 square miles; the London Telephone Area of over 1,000 square miles; and the London of the London Passenger Transport Board with its scarlet buses and trams running inside the County of London, its green buses outside the County and its Green Line coaches going out to places twenty or thirty miles away from the centre. But perhaps the strangest London of all is one that grew up during the Second World War, the Metropolitan Evacuation Area. At first this was made up of the County of London and all those parts of Surrey, Essex, Middlesex and Kent whose children were evacuated with the L.C.C. schools; but later such places as Swansea, Southampton, Birmingham and Yarmouth were included, because children from all these places were mixed up in the country districts and it was found convenient to treat them for some purposes as though they all came from the same place. So you see how difficult it is to say exactly what London is. People a hundred years ago found it just as difficult as we do. I have an old book in which the writer is talking about just this same difficulty. "A few years ago," he says, "the Justices for Middlesex wanted a new Courthouse, and so they built one in Clerkenwell, just on the edge of London; now that is right inside and to find the end of the town we must go to Tyburn." Tyburn is the place we now call the Marble Arch and all of you who have ever been to Hyde Park will know whether that is the end of London now. Perhaps the best way of deciding what is the real London to-day will be for us to see how London began and how it has grown. Then we may be able to settle how large it shall be in the future and whether there really is any way of keeping it to a reasonable size.

Let us look first of all at the London area before there

were any houses ; then we will try to imagine what the
first settlements were like, to see why London began
just where it did ; and, after that, we will trace its growth
from a little place not so big as many of our country
villages up to the great London of to-day, with its millions
of houses and a population larger than that of many of
the smaller countries of Europe.   To get a good picture
we will go out to Epsom Downs and look north.   If it is a
clear day we shall see in the distance the dim outline of
the hills to the north of London.   You know that Epsom
Downs are chalk, and perhaps you know that the hills to
the north of London are chalk too.   Now imagine that
you are standing on the edge of a great basin made of
chalk with a deep crack in its edge away to your right and
another not quite so deep opposite to it on your left.
Nearly fill your basin with clay, sand and gravel so that
patches of each show as lumps on the surface which
slopes gently down to a groove in the middle running
across and joining the cracks.   You will have a very good
idea of the kinds of soil and the slopes of the land on
which our London stands, the London Basin as we call it.
Now if you will imagine a river running in the groove
from one crack to the other and many smaller streams
going down to join it from the edges, if you can picture
the land covered with trees, dense forest on the clay
patches, lighter woodland on the gravels and marshy
places along the lower parts of the rivers, you can see
London before the houses appeared.   The dense forest
was full of wild boar and bears, almost impassable because
it was choked with a mass of brambles and thorns ; but
on the lighter gravels, where the woods were more open,
deer roamed, and there was good hunting, whilst the
streams gave good fishing.   So we can now imagine our
basin dotted with little villages, some in the light woods
on the upper parts of the streams, others on the gravel
patches down by the main river.   Joining these villages,
but keeping away from both the dense forest and the
marshes, there were trackways which we will study in a

later chapter. They are very interesting because they became first the Roman Roads and then the lines of our own main roads and railways. Just now, however, I want you to look at three of them. One is that which runs along the high ground from Canterbury, across Kent to Shooters Hill and then over Blackheath towards Westminster, where it crosses the Thames and goes away to the north-west along what is now the Edgware Road. Another runs from north-east to south-west, coming in from Colchester, crossing the Lea at Old Ford, and running north of the city by Old Street and on by an almost straight line to the Thames, which it crosses at Staines. The third comes in from the north, keeping as far as possible to the high land and the gravels, crosses the river at London Bridge and then goes away south by the road through Kennington, Clapham and Balham. I have tried to show all this on the map and if you will look at this you will see that a very little diversion would make them all cross just about the centre of the City of London and not far from London Bridge. If, as seems very likely was the case two thousand years ago, the tide came no higher up the river than here, this would be the spot where merchants from the Continent, if there were any, would settle for trade with the natives ; especially as the tracks spread away to all those parts of the country from which the important trade goods came in those days.

On either side of the Thames there are hard patches ; but in only one place are they just opposite one another, and that is about where London Bridge is now. There, on the south side, is a dry gravel patch, across which two of the tracks must go and just opposite to this are three low hills, Ludgate Hill, Cornhill and Tower Hill, with a good anchorage at the head of the tide and a sheltered harbour in the mouth of the Walbrook, a stream that still runs into the Thames by the side of Cannon Street Station but is now merely a sewer. If you were merchants from Europe looking for a good place to start

a trading station, you could not find a better in the whole
of Britain; it was easy to get at, easy to defend and
sheltered from all winds; and so you would probably
make it your chief centre. To it all the trade in Britain
would flow, to be collected and shipped to Europe; it
was a place where all the trade of the world outside
Europe and all the trade of Europe met and crossed; it
was, in fact, just what London is to-day and what she
has been right through her history.

Here is the first London about which we know anything
definite, the place that was burned by the tribesmen of
the Iceni and of which remains have been found. This
is the London that has grown into the great world capital
of to-day. Its remains are few, just some red pavements
up by the Walbrook where the Mansion House now
stands, a little burnt rubbish, and London Stone which
you may see set into the wall of St. Swithin's church in
Cannon Street but which used to be set into the ground
opposite. This stone is very old; Henry Fitzalwyn, the
first Mayor, is said to have lived near to it; and in Wren's
day it was surrounded by the buried remains of Roman
buildings; so that it is probably the actual centre of
London, the " miliarium " from which all distances were
measured on the Roman Roads. We have already seen
what happened to this first London, how it was destroyed
in A.D. 60, but was soon rebuilt and surrounded by the
wall that fixed the size of Roman and Medieval London.

The Roman town did not at first fill up all the area
inside the walls. There was a wide space kept entirely
free from buildings and a still wider space in which the
buildings were large; but as in all other Roman towns,
there was a great market place and a town hall near the
centre of the town. From this town hall main roads
went out as nearly at right angles as possible, cutting
the town up into four blocks which were further cut by
smaller roads, streets and lanes into islands, large in the
northern parts but small and crowded with houses down
by the river. Outside the wall to a depth of nearly half

a mile in width were the cemeteries; across the bridge, in Southwark, there was a settlement of inns and lodgings for travellers and other strangers who were not allowed to sleep in the city itself. No traces of any Roman villages have been found in the country immediately around London and only a few country houses (villas), so that there were probably very few settlers except in the city itself. London grew in importance but not in size during the four centuries of Roman occupation. Then for nearly a century it is lost altogether, and it does not seem to have regained its leading position until the middle of the seventh century when it had a bishop and was an English town. We can only guess what happened. Probably, as the English settled in the country around and cut off trade, the people gradually left London, its houses fell down, grass grew in the streets and everything was lost in a wilderness of ruins except the wall and a few crowded lanes down by the river. During this time the English were filling up the country around London, dotting it with farm settlements and little villages that have grown into the metropolitan boroughs of to-day; but they kept away from the city and they kept away from the great cemeteries, and so we do not find any of their villages closer than a mile away. As the country settled down Frankish traders came across and settled in London, the English themselves went in as merchants and work-men, and London began to grow once more.

For a long time growth was slow, for the space inside the walls was too big for the people who wanted to live there; they crowded once more into the narrow space by the river. A few foreign merchants set up houses along the line of Cheapside and the space north of this was filled with monasteries and the houses of those Saxon nobles who came to live in London. Then, when the Danish invasion began, the walls were repaired, the city was defended and the Danes themselves came to settle in it as peaceful merchants bringing much trade from the Baltic coasts. They were soon joined by merchants from

Italy and France and once more London began to grow. This time it soon spread beyond the walls, for monasteries were set up all round London just outside the walls; bishops and abbots from the country built town houses along Fleet Street and in Southwark, and with the great Abbey of St. Peter and the Royal Palace nearby at Westminster, the great nobles began to build along the Strand. At the same time the little English villages grew, for there was a great demand for all the farm produce they could spare to feed the people in the city and at the Court; travellers and pilgrims began to use the roads and more people came to live in London itself. During the thirteenth century some of the trades like soap, glue and candle-making were sent outside the walls because of the smell and the risk of fire, and houses for the workers were built along the banks of the Fleet river and outside Bishopsgate and Aldgate, whilst there was more building along the river east of the Tower for the people who worked on the ships and for the foreign sailors who were not allowed to sleep in the city. But for a long time London did not grow much outside the walls although the number of people increased rapidly. There was still a good deal of vacant space inside the walled area, and the increase of population was taken up by building houses of several stories and crowding many people into one house. By the middle of the fifteenth century, however, London was getting so busy that it could not find room for all the people who had work there, and so they began to build outside. Even so late as the middle of the reign of Henry VIII, however, Stepney is spoken of as a pleasant country village to which the citizens walked across the fields on Sunday afternoons. By the end of that reign, houses had covered the sites of nearly all the monasteries outside the walls.

The first suburbs were Southwark, Smithfields and Finsbury. Southwark had been a suburb ever since Roman times, for it was a convenient place for travellers to stay when they came in from the Continent ; but now it began to fill up, and houses were built along the Bankside where the theatres were, and out towards Bermondsey, already becoming famous for its leather. At Smithfield was the Priory and Hospital of St. Bartholomew. The monks had an annual horse and cattle fair and a permanent cloth fair and these drew from all parts of Europe a great many people and for them there were inns and lodgings ; thus a crowded suburb had grown up there which was extended eastwards to Finsbury and round to Aldgate where new industries, silk-weaving, paper-making and others, were set up in Tudor times. At the same time Westminster was growing, for when Parliament and the Court came to live there permanently and the Law Courts were settled in Westminster Hall, houses had to be built for all the people who were drawn there. London had begun to grow and nothing could stop it. The Government tried, for they were afraid of what might happen if too many people were crowded together in a small space, and especially were they afraid of the spread of disease, of the dangers of starvation and of rioting. So proclamations were made and Acts of Parliament passed ordering that London should stop growing, but they might as well have tried to stop a healthy boy from growing ; it could not be done. London was alive and Acts of Parliament will not stop

St. Bartholomew the Great, Smithfield

live things from growing. The Proclamation of 1581 shows what they feared. . . .

for that such great multitudes of people inhabiting small rooms, whereof many be so poor that they must live by begging and being heaped up together and in a sort smothered with many families and children in one house or small tenement it follows that if any sort of plague or general sickness come among them it would immediately spread through the whole City.

So they made it unlawful to build any new house within three miles of either London or Westminster or to divide any existing house up into flats, and they ordered that any empty house that was less than seven years old should be pulled down. But they allowed the gentry to have licences to build new houses for themselves and these houses were turned into flats twenty years later when their owners had got tired of them and wanted to move a little farther out. Besides, when people had to live near London, and more and more people were coming in as new trades were set up, houses had to be found and this was done by converting barns and sheds into houses and flats and by adding more stories to houses already there. So, in Shakespeare's time, all the vacant spaces in the city had been built on and there were continuous blocks of houses back to Chancery Lane and round the north and east sides of the city, whilst there was ribbon development along the river to Rotherhithe and Poplar and back along the main roads for over a mile. But the whole of South London was still open country ; Bethnal Green, Hackney and Islington were a long way from town, St. Martin's and St. Giles were really in the fields ; Long Acre was a country lane and Covent Garden a vegetable garden instead of a market. Places like Chelsea or Kensington were so far away that most Londoners had never seen them, although they might have heard of them.

When James I was king a new sort of house was beginning to be built, using brick instead of timber, and with a flush front like ours instead of the old overhanging upper stories. " London," said King James, " is changing from sticks to bricks," and this change was encouraged because there was less risk of fire ; but it meant more people coming to London, for brickyards had to be set up to make bricks from the London brickearth and these employed more men than the timber trades had done.

Both Charles I and Cromwell tried to stop London's growth, Charles by Acts forbidding new building and Cromwell by the far more sensible plan of ordering that every new house built in the country around London should have three acres of land attached to it. If this had been done modern London would not be nearly so crowded as it is, but, unfortunately, the Plague and the Fire ruined the plan. During the Plague thousands of people got away from the city and had to be accommodated in the country ; then, just as they were coming back, the Fire burned down most of the houses and the people had to stay out until new houses were built. At first they lived in tents ; then wooden huts were built for them ; and gradually these were replaced by permanent houses. Some of these were in the villages and little towns of the London area ; but the poorer people and the workmen who were rebuilding the city had to live near their work, and so crowded streets of small houses were built in Whitechapel and along the lanes behind Holborn and Fleet Street. All this building was quite without plan. Outside the city it was nobody's business, and so people who owned a little piece of land just ran up as many houses as they could on it ; but in the city some attempt was made to replan. Sir Christopher Wren and others produced plans for a fine city ; but, whilst they were talking, London's business had to go on, and so people rebuilt their houses and shops on the old sites and the city was just as crowded as before, although there were fewer people living there and the streets looked wider because the new houses had straight fronts. Amongst the plans was a very interesting one for a Greater London, an oval shaped area extending from Limehouse to Chelsea and back from the river for about two miles on each side. It was to be surrounded by a wall and the people who made the plan suggested that this wall could be used for growing fruits such as pears and peaches, a fine idea if it could have been carried out. But it was not done, perhaps because the idea was in advance of its time; and London just grew with nobody caring how.

During the eighteenth century London grew even more rapidly. South of the river people lived as far out as Camberwell and Kennington; the district of St. George's Fields was built over; and by the end of the century the boundary was City Road, Euston Road and Marylebone Road in the north, Park Lane and on to the river at Vauxhall in the west, whilst there were houses as far as Poplar in the east and along the river and out to Bethnal Green in the north-east. The most interesting part of this building was in Bloomsbury where the land was owned by the great families of Bedford and Russell, who planned the lay-out of the ground before they allowed any building and insisted that the houses should not be built in rows but round the sides of a square with an open space in the middle. The building of squares had started in the seventeenth century with St. James's Square and Lincoln's Inn Fields, followed by Soho and Leicester Square. Towards the end of the century Red Lion Square and Queen Square, Holborn had been built, the latter with its north side open so that the Princess Anne, whose house (now the Bloomsbury Trade School) was on the south side, could look out to the country. Then, in the time of Queen Anne and George I, the Bloomsbury squares were laid out, first those near the Foundling Hospital and then those around what is now the British Museum. Then came the squares of Bayswater and Mayfair, followed at the beginning of the nineteenth century by those of Belgravia and later by the buildings north and south of Hyde Park and Kensington Gardens. All these districts were laid out for wealthy people and the houses were beautifully built with lovely patterned plaster ceilings, carved marble mantels and fireplaces in the Adam style, so called because it was first introduced by the Adam brothers, four Scottish architects who became famous when they designed the Adelphi (the word means " brothers "). This building around a square became very fashionable. There are many squares in other parts of London and in other cities too, but no place in the world has so fine a group of them as London. During the first half of the nineteenth century the growth of factories in the country just outside London and along the banks of the Thames and the Lea gave rise to another type of building. Thousands of little cottages were set up for the workers in the new factories. If the squares are some of the finest in the world, the miles of little cottages in little drab streets are some of the most ugly ; and unfortunately it is these that the traveller to London sees most of, for his train passes level with their roofs for miles. The factories brought them first, but the railways themselves brought more in the districts like New Cross, Clapham Junction and Kentish Town, where dismal streets of ugly little cottages were built for the railway workers. As a rule they are not quite so bad as the back-to-back cottages of most of the northern industrial towns, for the London workmen's houses did generally have a bit of garden, and most of them are set back a few feet from the footpath with another bit of garden behind railings. It is their sameness that makes them so ugly— thousands of them all exactly alike—without even a tree to break the monotony of the lines of street. All this building meant still more people, for the hundreds of thousands of workers had to be fed, and this meant more shops and transport, more water and gas, more traffic on the roads and still more people ; for as the population grew more had to come in to supply its needs. This meant a great increase in the number of shopkeepers, clerks and others who wanted rather better houses and could afford the time and money for travelling. So for them, in the last half of the century, long rows of houses, looking much like the rows of workmen's cottages, only rather bigger, with longer gardens back and front and with trees lining the roads, were built in Streatham, Lewisham and other places a little farther out ; a rather nicer sort of monotony but still monotony, for again they were all the same pattern, thousands and thousands of them. So now all the pleasant little villages were swallowed up by houses, and as more workmen were wanted in the inner part and no more cottages could be built, great blocks of drab-looking flats were built, of dull brick and painted a dirty brown so that they looked worse than they really were, although the people who lived in them generally did their best to brighten them up a bit with boxes of flowering plants on the window-sills and a few scarlet geraniums in the windows. For the true Londoner loves colour and hates drabness ; so he usually does something to brighten things up even in the most dismal surroundings.

In the twentieth century quicker means of transport were invented—electric trams, motor buses and tube railways—and people went farther out, always trying to live on the edge of the country so that they could have a garden and see some trees ; for London people like gardens and green trees although they do not care to live in the real country because it seems too slow for them.

Now houses began to appear in the fields of Eltham and Epsom, up the river to Hampton Court, south to Coulsdon and north to Barnet ; for what really decides how far out we can live is how far we can go in an hour without having to start much before eight in the morning. Two hundred years ago when everybody walked, except the rich people who had their carriages, the distance was about two miles ; but then there were so few people that nearly everyone could live where he worked, often upstairs over the shop or workshop. A hundred years ago, when most people still walked but a good many either rode their own horses or came by horse-drawn buses, the distance was from two to five miles. Fifty years ago horse-trams, bicycles and steam trains had sent the distance up to anything from eight to twelve miles. To-day the motor bus and the tube train have sent it up to anything from twelve to twenty miles for most people, whilst those who have their own cars can live up to thirty miles from their work. To-morrow the aerobus may take us to work a hundred or more miles away in an hour, and we shall perhaps live that far away and find that the whole of the present London area has become what the city is to-day, a mass of offices, and the country up to a hundred miles away one mass of houses, unless we can find some way of stopping this from happening. Perhaps one way will be for us to build pleasant blocks of flats to live in on the two or three days that we have to work and to have country cottages in garden towns a hundred miles away in which to live for the rest of the week.

So there is a problem for you to solve; how to stop London from growing so big that it will fill all the country for a hundred miles around, without killing it. For the world needs a London where people live as well as work, because an inhabited London stands for so much that the world must have : fine thoughts that can only come from many people living together in one sort of life, literature, art and music; all these things would be lost if London became just one big office and workshop, and we all lived in little communities of a few thousand people and consequently thought little local thoughts. Many people are thinking about this problem, but not all are thinking wisely. Some are jealous of London and would like to see it made much smaller and less important, and others have not yet studied its history and so found out how it grew in the past and why it is still growing.

Many plans have been suggested for improving London without either destroying its importance or allowing it to spread over all the nearby country. One of the most important of these is the *County of London Plan*.

CHAPTER IV

LONDON'S ROADS AND TRAFFIC

ONE of the most troublesome of all London's problems is the traffic. Every year London's streets become more crowded, and although we make new plans for speeding up the traffic and getting the roads clear, the only result seems to be that we get more and more vehicles on the roads, especially in the centre of London, so that it becomes increasingly difficult to get about. Every year, too, London gets larger and larger, and so more and more people have to travel, which makes the problem worse.

The real trouble is that London is a centre through which practically all the traffic from north to south and from east to west must go, and the two streams hold up each other and cause congestion that is made worse by the local traffic of London itself. If you look at a physical map of the south-east of England you will see at once why this is. London is situated at the very best place for crossing southern England, either from east to west or from north to south, so that all the traffic must cross in the London area. That is really the reason why London exists at all. It is there because it is a natural traffic crossing and it has grown for the same reason. The lower Thames valley is almost surrounded by hills through which the river breaks at Reading. In these hills there are passes through which all the roads must go and all these passes point to the London area. The sketchmap on page 69 will make this clear.

If you will look at a map of the Roman roads in Britain—you will find one in any history book—and then compare it with the modern main roads and the railways, you will see that they all use these gaps in the hills, for even where the hills are only a few hundred feet high the passes are just as important for traffic as they are in really mountainous country, and the road routes follow them just as carefully. The Roman town was built just where the north to south roads crossed the east to west routes, and for many centuries this was the only point where they could cross the river; so London Bridge was always the most important crossing. The Roman city had wide straight roads crossing it at right angles to each other, and smaller streets also crossing at right angles; so it would have been fairly easy to get about in it. When the English came the roads were no longer used, except for two which seem to have continued in use right through Saxon times, and both of these passed through London. The road from Aldgate through Cheapside to Newgate and the one from the bridge northwards to Bishopsgate have always been the two main roads of the city of London, and still form two of the most important routes through modern London.

Medieval London grew up anyhow, with narrow crowded lanes winding down to the river, and it must have been very difficult to get about in it, for it was very congested. There were no coaches, it is true, but all the more important people and many of the others too rode on horseback; and there were waggons for the goods. If these waggons could get through the gateways they must have blocked the narrow lanes completely just as lorries do to-day. If you want a good idea of the difficulty of getting about medieval London, walk along Thames Street from the Tower to Blackfriars and you will know what it must have been like, for it is just the same width now as it was then and is probably just as crowded. Although there are more lorries to-day, each takes up less room than the old waggons did with their teams of great Flemish horses.

Fortunately for themselves the Londoners of the Middle Ages could use the Thames, for the river was wide and safe and everyone travelled by boat. The King, the great nobles whose palaces lined the Strand, and the bishops all had their barges; so had the Lord

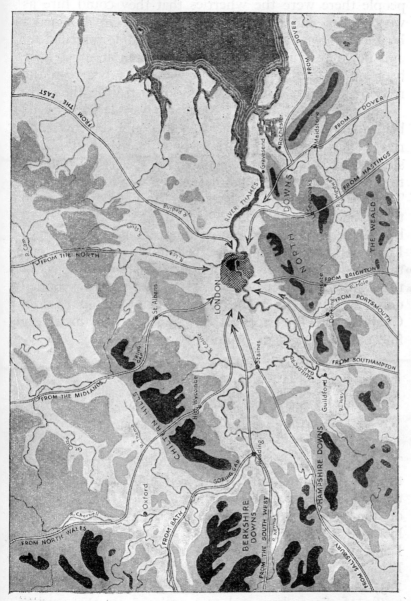

ALL ROADS LEAD TO LONDON

Mayor, the aldermen and the guilds, whilst for ordinary people there were the wherries that they could hire as we do taxis, and no doubt many of the people owned a boat as we own cars or bicycles. So people travelled up and down by water, and a pleasant sight it must have been on a summer evening to watch the boats on the river or to go for a row as we go for a stroll in the park.

For centuries London's transport was decided by its bridge, for London Bridge was the only one over the river so far down, and there was not another until Kingston, which was too far away from the great road running to the north to be of much use except as a local crossing. There was probably a bridge across the Thames in Roman times, and there may have been one even before then, but if there was we know nothing about it. The first London Bridge of which we have any record is the one that crossed the river by Botolph's Wharf in the days of the Danish invasions. This is the one that was pulled down by Olaf the Norseman in 1014, as you read in Chapter II. The story of this attack is told in a very fine old Norse poem beginning :

> London Bridge is broken down,
> Gold is won and bright renown ;
> Shields resounding : warhorns sounding,
> Hildur shouting in the din,
> Arrows singing, mailcoats ringing,
> Odin makes our Olaf win.

The bridge was soon rebuilt, only to be destroyed several times again, sometimes by fire and sometimes by flood ; until in 1176 Peter of Colechurch decided to build one of stone a little farther up the river. Peter died before his work was completed and it was finished by three London merchants. This was the famous old London Bridge of which you often see pictures, and it lasted until 1831, when it became too weak to carry the heavier traffic of those days and was replaced by the present bridge, which has since had to be widened to take the still heavier traffic of to-day. This old bridge was

LONDON BRIDGE BEFORE THE FIRE OF 1632

(*After an engraving by Visscher, showing the Medieval and Tudor houses which occupied the whole of the bridge at this time*)

guarded against disaster by three famous Saints: St. Olaf, whose church stood at the Southwark end; St. Magnus, who guarded the northern end; and St. Thomas Becket, who had a chapel on the middle of the bridge. The arches were so narrow and the piers between them so wide that they acted as a dam, forming a wide lake above bridge and dangerous rapids which wise travellers avoided, landing and walking round whilst their boatmen shot the rapids.   Sometimes a traveller would risk the rapids and many people were drowned in attempting the passage, although some were lucky enough to be washed up on to the wooden platforms that had been built to protect the piers.   These people usually had to be hauled up by the cranes in the houses above like bales of goods. Houses were built on the bridge soon after it was finished, and in spite of the crowding of the roadway and the danger of fires these houses were not pulled down until the middle of the eighteenth century.

The whole life of England went either over or under London Bridge.   Almost from its beginning there were parties of pilgrims crossing it on their way to the shrine of St. Thomas at Canterbury ; they began their journey with prayers for protection in St. Thomas's chapel on the bridge and they ended it, if they were lucky, in the chapel of St. Thomas in the cathedral at Canterbury. Over the bridge went merchants from all parts of England to the great wool markets of Flanders, soldiers to or from the French Wars, great nobles both English and foreign, bishops and abbots, Plantagenet Kings to fight the French, peasants to sell their vegetables in the London markets, royal and noble prisoners, knights, squires and yeomen, citizens and craftsmen—all adding something to the gay and busy scene.

At the time of the Peasant Revolt a fierce battle was fought on the bridge between the citizens and the Kentishmen under Wat Tyler, and a few years later there was a great tournament between the Scottish knight, Sir David Lindsey and the English noble, Lord Welles.   The Scot sat his horse so well that the people said he was tied on to his saddle, and to show them that he was not, he jumped off and on again.   In the third round he struck Lord Welles so hard that the Englishman was thrown from his horse like a stone from a sling and the

Scot made himself very popular with the crowd by getting down from his horse and running to render first aid to his fallen foe. Over the bridge rode the Black Prince after Poictiers, with the French King John as his prisoner. Over it too came Henry V with his victorious army after Agincourt, escorted by the Lord Mayor, the aldermen and the liverymen of the guilds all in their robes, the bishop and the clergy in rich copes. This was a Londoner's triumph, for a large part of the victorious army had been London men. A few years later the bridge saw the funeral procession of Henry, on its way to Westminster Abbey.

Over this bridge too passed Henry VIII and Wolsey fresh from the Field of the Cloth of Gold, Philip of Spain to his wedding with Mary Tudor, and Elizabeth from her progresses in Kent and Surrey. Charles II passed across it on his return from his exile in Holland; across it streamed the fugitives from the Plague and the Fire, and over it went all the travellers to and from the Continent during the eighteenth century. So they pass: Roman soldiers from their camps to the stations on the Wall, Saxon and Dane fighting for the city, soldiers for the French wars or pilgrims bound for Canterbury. Then in the early years of the last century the old bridge was replaced by the new one, to be used by the new traffic. City merchants on horseback and their clerks on foot used it when it was new; their successors in cars and buses use it to-day.

Once it was the only bridge within the London area; even to-day, with a dozen others to help, it still carries a constant stream of lorries, buses and cars in the road-way, of clerks and typists on its footways. Only on Sundays does the traffic slacken.

The medieval bridge was closed by gates and over the one on the Southwark side were placed the heads of those who had been executed for treason. The first head was that of Sir William Wallace, the Scottish patriot, and the last those of the rebels of the '45.

But if the old bridge saw its pageants and its tragedies, it also had its romances. In 1536 a baby girl fell from the window of one of the houses on the bridge into the river below. She would have been swept away by the current and drowned but for one of her father's apprentices, Thomas Osborne, who dived into the rapids and saved the child. Both grew up and many young nobles wanted to marry the girl, for she was both beautiful and rich, but her father would not allow her to marry any of them. "No," he said, "the lad saved her life and he alone shall marry her." So, when she was eighteen, they were married, and some years later Osborne, now Sir Thomas, became Lord Mayor.

No other bridges were built across the river in the London area until the middle of the eighteenth century, although many proposals had been made for another to relieve the congestion on London Bridge. But the plans were always opposed by the watermen who were very numerous and powerful, and who feared they would lose much of their trade if more bridges were built. At last Westminster had become so crowded with nobles and gentry, who wanted to cross without taking the long journey through the city, or running the risks of the horse ferry at Lambeth, that a new bridge was built just by the Houses of Parliament, where the river is actually wider than it is at London Bridge. After this, as London grew larger and larger, more bridges were built: Blackfriars in 1760 (called Pitt Bridge in honour of the Earl of Chatham), Waterloo Bridge (called Strand Bridge) in 1817, then a number of others farther up the river, the Tower Bridge in 1894, and the new Waterloo Bridge in 1944. All the bridges of London have been rebuilt or widened during the last century. You will remember how Waterloo Bridge became unsafe, and, being already too narrow for the traffic that went over it, was rebuilt, and actually finished during the Second World War, in spite of the German air raids. There are still not enough crossings to carry all London's traffic over the river and there are plans for more bridges and tunnels. The new bridges will probably be taken across the river at high level, carrying the traffic right over the Embankment and the Strand and not coming down to surface level until they are well away from the river.

It was the spread of London and the introduction of coaches, both occurring during the time of Queen Elizabeth, that really began our modern traffic problems. In the days of James I coaches became common and began to ply for hire, much to the disgust of the watermen, one of whom, John Taylor, who was something of a poet, wrote :

> 'Tis not fit that
> Fulsom madams and new scurvy squires
> Should jolt the streets at their desires
> Like great triumphal Tamburlaines,
> Drawn with the pampered steeds of Belgia
> That almost all the streets are choked with them.

In another book he says, this time in prose :

"Look into the streets about Flete Street and the Strand and see how they are pestered with them (the coaches) . . . where the earth quakes and trembles, the casements shatter, tatter and chatter and such a noise is heard that a man can neither sleep, speak, hear, write or eat his dinner in peace for them."

I wonder what Taylor would have said about the traffic had he been living to-day ? The

AN EIGHTEENTH CENTURY LADY IN A SEDAN CHAIR

coaches were great clumsy affairs and they found the London streets very inconvenient, so that they were used only in the wider roads, whilst for getting about in the town itself, especially in the fashionable quarters, the sedan chair was far more convenient as the chairmen could carry it right into the house and the ladies and gentlemen could go from one house to another without getting their clothes spoiled.

Travelling in London, even for those who could afford a coach or a chair, was far more difficult and dangerous than it is to-day. Here are some of the lines from Gay's *Trivia*, a poem written in the eighteenth century, which show how unpleasant it could be :

> I've seen a beau, in some ill-fated hour,
> When o'er the stones choked kennels swell the shower
> In gilded chariot loll : he with disdain
> Views spattered passengers all drenched with rain.
> With mud filled high the rumbling cart draws near,
> Now rule thy prancing steeds laced charioteer;
> The dustman lashes on with spiteful rage,
> His ponderous spokes thy painted wheel engage,
> Crushed in thy pride down falls the shrieking beau,
> The slabby pavement crystal fragments strew,
> Black floods of mire th' embroidered coat disgrace,
> And mud enwraps the honours of his face.

People, however, were travelling more : the London merchants from their new country houses at Streatham or Clapham, the gentry from their great houses. Something had to be done to improve both coaches and roads ; so the last half of the eighteenth century is the great age of roadmaking. The new roads were called " turnpikes," and they were either made by commercial companies like our railways are to-day or they were under the control of groups of men called Turnpike Commissioners. In any case those who used the roads had to pay for them by tolls. So that these could be collected, gates were set up and toll-keepers' cottages built. This system made far better roads than there had been even in London since the Romans left ; but as each road under one authority was short, the gates were frequent and travellers had to stop every few miles to pay the toll. Gradually the roads were taken over by the local authorities, but there are a few of the gatehouses left in London; names like New Cross Gate and Kennington Gate remind us where others were, and we still have one road that is closed by a tollgate and on which tolls have to be paid. This is at Dulwich, a real country village right in the heart of South London and only about four miles away from London Bridge.

The stage coaches carrying passengers and the faster mail coaches grew in number very rapidly as soon as good roads were made, and as their owners paid a fixed sum they did not have to stop for the toll gates; so it was much quicker to travel in this way and they soon became popular. In 1817 there were no fewer than 694 regular lines running from London daily, and they kept such good time that the country people used to set their clocks by them. Those of you who have read *Pickwick Papers* will remember how Mr. Pickwick used to travel by coach, although railways were then just beginning; and you will find many interesting descriptions of coach travel if you read stories written at the beginning of the nineteenth century. To get all this traffic in and out of London, and to get the gentlemen and the merchants about, meant that many new roads had to be made and many of the old roads widened. You can see these new roads in many parts of London. They were then almost in the country, but they are now right in the middle of London, because when they were made new houses were built along them like the ribbon development along our new arterial roads just before the war, so that more people wanted to travel to London and more roads had to be made. There were so many different authorities still controlling London that any sort of real improvement was hopeless, and so the Government decided to set up the Metropolitan Board of Works to take over all the matters that concerned the whole of the London area and were not merely local. One of the chief problems the Board had to solve was that of roads, and one of the finest pieces of work it did was to make the new road from the Mansion House to Westminster by way of Queen Victoria Street and the Embankment; whilst another was the building of Holborn Viaduct, to connect Cheapside with Holborn without traffic having to go down the steep slope of Snow Hill and up the other side. At the same time the various bridges across the Thames were freed from tolls so that it became much easier to get across the river.

For people who wanted to get about in London itself two new methods of transport came into use, the cab and the omnibus. There were two sorts of cab : the four-wheeler, usually called a " growler," perhaps because of the noise it made, possibly because the drivers grumbled about the smallness of their tips ; and the " hansom," named after its inventor. The growler was used for long journeys, especially by people with luggage, whilst the lighter hansom, with its driver perched up behind, was very popular in the West End and the heart of London for short journeys. A very dashing affair it was with its shining coachwork and the jingling of the harness and the bells on the horses' collars. A journey in a hansom was far more exciting than travelling by taxi is now, and somehow the horse seemed to travel very much faster. It always appeared something of an adventure too, especially as the driver had a little trapdoor in the roof through which he could see his passengers.

The omnibus was a sort of cab, only longer. It was introduced from Paris just over a century ago by a Mr. Shillibeer. He opened a bus route from Paddington to the Bank with one bus each way daily at a shilling fare ; but he made it much more interesting than bus rides are to-day by providing papers and magazines for his passengers to read ; they wanted something of the sort as the journey took nearly three hours. A little later another route was opened from Dulwich to the city, and others quickly followed, so that in a very short time

PICCADILLY CIRCUS IN THE 'NINETIES

there were several routes working and the fares had come down considerably. Only luggage was carried on top, but there seemed no limit to the number of passengers that could be squeezed inside. The conductors (they were called cads) would never admit that their bus was full and could always manage to get another passenger in. London very nearly got its first motor-bus about this time when a steam bus started running from the Bank to Paddington. It began at six miles an hour, but, when it had got going well and had up plenty of steam, the speed was increased to ten miles. The owners advertised that it was quite safe, could not be blown up, and that it could stop instantly. The authorities, however, refused to give it a licence, so that the idea was dropped until the beginning of the present century, when the coming of the petrol bus brought steam buses on the roads again, and the National Steam Car Company ran several routes in south-east and east London. The railways that were built at about the same time as buses were coming on the roads, are hardly a London concern; they were really intended more as a means of getting into and out of the Metropolis than for travelling in it, and at first they were kept well away from the centre. As London grew, lines were built joining up the new suburbs with each other and with the centre, but it was not until 1860 that anything was done to get people about in the heart of London by train. Then a Mr. Pearson suggested that a railway in a circular tunnel running round London should be built to link up main line stations, and after some years of talk the Metropolitan Railway was made from Liverpool Street Station round the north of the city to Paddington by way of St. Pancras and Euston. Then it went by South Kensington to Victoria and so under the Embankment and the city back to Liverpool Street, completing the circle. It was not really an underground railway, only a cutting roofed over, and, as the engines were driven by steam, the tunnel was always full of smoke. The third-class passengers, who at first had

ON AN UNDERGROUND RAILWAY ESCALATOR

to travel in open trucks as though they were goods, must have been very uncomfortable. Later it became very popular, and I can remember how we boys used to enjoy taking a ticket to the next station but getting there by going the wrong way and travelling right round the circle. Soon after the opening of the Circle another railway like it was made joining East Ham to Wimbledon and Harrow. The trains on this line, called the District, ran over the Circle rails for some distance. This brought many more places within easy reach of the centre, but did very little to relieve the pressure there, which was made worse when the Tubes came into use. The first of these was the City and South London from Clapham Common, followed soon by the Twopenny Tube, running from Shepherd's Bush to the Bank with only

F

one fare, twopence for any distance. As the trains were driven by electric power these tube lines were much more comfortable than the old Underground, and as they were quick and the trains very frequent they became very popular. Besides the tubes, there were the trams, now being replaced by trolley-buses. The first tram route ran from Marble Arch to Paddington in 1860, but it took another ten years before trams were really established. After that the number of routes increased until the L.C.C. took them over at the beginning of the present century. The old horse-drawn trams were abolished and electric trams put in their places, fares were lowered, and the time taken on the journeys shortened. Before the L.C.C. took over the trams they were owned by a large number of companies and the routes were short and disconnected, but one of the first things the Council did was to link up all the routes, join those north of the Thames with those on the south by a line over Westminster Bridge and under Kingsway, and to link their routes with those just outside London so that really long journeys could be taken.

As there was still a great deal of confusion in London's passenger transport, the London Passenger Transport Board was set up in 1933 to take over the whole of the passenger transport except that carried by the suburban lines of the great railways. So now we find it very easy to get about London; we can travel in comfort and quite quickly and cheaply. There is still a lot to be done to make travel in London really speedy and cheap, and some plan will have to be found to relieve the congestion in the centre, perhaps by building new high-level roads from south to north, crossing over the existing east to west routes and confined to fast through traffic; perhaps more of the traffic will go underground or even into the air. Sir Charles Bressey's report, *Highway Development*, 1937 (*Greater London*), made some suggestions for solving the traffic problem. These suggestions included high-level crossings at such places as Ludgate Circus,

Trafalgar Square and the Elephant and Castle, where very heavy traffic streams cross each other. The report also suggested various new through routes and many other road improvements.

But the Bressey Plan deals only with roads and is concerned chiefly with the task of getting vehicles through London without the many delays that are now caused by the crowded crossings. It takes little notice of the other problems caused by the great size of London and the number of people who live there. Yet it is on their solution that that of the traffic problem really depends.

There are, in fact, three main problems to be solved in connection with London's road traffic. One is the question of getting people into and out of the centre of London quickly and easily, especially in the morning and evening rush hours when all the business people are either going to their work or going home. Very large numbers have to travel at these times and they all want to get about as quickly and cheaply as possible. In the evening, too, there are great crowds who want to get to and from the places of entertainment in the West End. All these people want to be moved without interfering with the other traffic that is on the roads at the same time. Then there is the local traffic, to and from offices and factories in the different parts of London during the day, and there are the crowds who travel from their homes to the main shopping centres. In addition to this there are all the people arriving at the great railway stations and crossing from one to the other or going to their homes. There is a vast amount of traffic to and from the docks and the great railway goods yards, in from the country to the markets and out from the central markets to the shops in the suburbs. There is also a great deal of traffic that must pass through London from one part of the country to another. Much of this can go by rail, but quite a lot has to go by road and must pass through some part of the London area even if it can be made to miss the city and the crowded central districts.

The real difficulty is to get through traffic across London without interfering with London's own traffic, to sort out and separate fast-moving streams from those that go more slowly and to separate the local traffic from that which is going some distance. Such purely local traffic as the tradesman's delivery van is very little trouble ; it uses side roads and only goes short distances. It is the area traffic that is the real bother because it uses the same main roads as the fast stream, but is constantly turning into or out of these roads, slowing up the faster vehicles whilst it crosses the road. So the problem for the road engineers and the traffic controllers is to find a way of sorting out the various streams and sending each on its way without it interfering with the others.

The *County of London Plan* proposes to deal with this difficulty in a simple but effective way. It first of all tries to sort out the roads according to the different kinds of traffic stream that each has to carry, keeping each stream, as far as possible, to one kind of road, and running the main roads between residential and business areas rather than through them. In this way each district would be kept free from fast, non-stop traffic, and its own roads would only carry the traffic that was actually serving premises in the area. The main roads carrying traffic from one district to another would run between the areas, separating them from each other but connecting them together.

Then there are the great through roads radiating from the river crossings and carrying traffic right across London, or right through it from one part of the country to another. These roads have to carry a great variety as well as a great volume of traffic : fast vehicles carrying passengers across London from one side to the other, traffic into and out of the centre and heavy but slow goods to and from the docks and markets. To relieve the pressure on these roads the planners suggest four ring roads. One of these is a railroad and would carry most of the heavy stuff from the docks, but the others

TRAFFIC CENTRE AT CANNON STREET

are ordinary roads going round London at various distances from the centre and linking up with the radial roads at various points.

The innermost ring would run round at about two miles out from Trafalgar Square and would give communication between the different parts of Central London without any unnecessary crossing of the central area ; the outer ring, running in the south almost round the County boundary but in the north being well outside the County, would distribute traffic to the outer areas without sending it through the centre. The important ring is the middle one, running round some four miles out. This would be a very wide main road designed to take fast and slow traffic in different streams. It would join up the docks and the industrial areas of East London with the more purely residential districts of the north, west and south. It would save much of the present congestion in the central districts because it would connect with the radial roads at some distance out. To get traffic across London it is suggested that two great routes should be used, one running from north to south from Swiss Cottage to the Elephant and Castle where it would fork, one part going south through Clapham and the other south-east. The east to west route would enter the city by Aldgate, run along an embankment on the site of Thames Street and the present Embankment to Waterloo Bridge, where it would go underground by way of St. James's Park to Victoria Station. Here it would come to the surface once more and go away to the south-west.

All these roads would cross the others and link up with them by overpasses, underpasses and various kinds of junction and roundabout. In this way London's traffic would be sorted out and distributed, and delays would be avoided because slow-moving vehicles would be taken off the roads used by the faster traffic. It is a plan that should go a long way towards solving London's traffic problems.

CHAPTER V

THE HOLE IN THE ROAD

TOM and Bill were going to school one morning when they heard the sound of pneumatic drills, and so they went along to see what was happening. They found that a piece of the street had been roped off and that inside this space men were busy breaking up the road. The boys had not time to wait and see why the road was being opened, for just then the bell began to ring and they had to hurry off to school. All through the morning they could hear the rattle of the drills and when morning school was over they ran round again to see what the men had been doing. They soon discovered what was wrong, for some of the men had now fitted up a pump and were pumping water from a big hole under the road, whilst others were digging a trench along the road from the hole they had first opened. One of the water mains had burst, and the water had washed out a big cavity under the surface of the road. The water had now been shut off and the men were clearing the hole and getting out the piece of broken pipe so that they could fit in a new length. The boys saw that there were many other sets of pipes under the road besides the water main ; there were telephone and telegraph wires, electric light cables, gas mains, and some earthenware pipes running from each house to join a larger pipe that ran down the length of the street at a lower level than all the others. Some men were digging down to this and the boys found that it was the sewer which the men were exposing in order to see if it had been damaged by the water from the burst main. It was all very exciting and the boys watched for some days until all the work was finished, the hole filled in, the road surface mended by the workmen from the Borough Council and everything had been cleared away. They had almost forgotten all about it when one day their History Master began to talk about London's water supply. He started his lesson by reminding them of the burst water main and how the water supply for the school had been cut off for a whole day; from this they went on to talk about the way London used to get its water and how it is supplied to-day. The boys were surprised to find how much water is used in London each day and what a big task it is supplying and purifying it all. To store one day's supply of water for London would need a tank two and a half times the size of Trafalgar Square and so deep that Nelson on the top of his column would be under water. To keep this supply flowing day by day immense reservoirs have been built, so big that they hold enough water for a hundred days if no more were pumped in. The largest of these is the Queen Mary reservoir at Littleton, just above Hampton Court. It is the biggest artificial lake in the world and is just about the size of Kensington Gardens, Hyde Park, the Green Park and St. James's Park added together. In addition to this there are square miles of storage reservoirs where the water is kept when it is first taken from the Thames, acres of filter beds where it is cleaned and purified, a hundred service reservoirs where the filtered water is kept for use and nearly eight thousand miles of mains. Three hundred great pumping engines are used to force the water along the mains and up to the top stories of London's tall buildings. Most of the water is taken from the Thames just above Teddington, but some of it comes from the River Lea and some from the New River, an artificial stream that brings water from springs in Hertfordshire. The south-eastern part of London gets its water from artesian wells going deep down into the chalk that underlies London, but all the sources of supply are connected so that if one of them should fail the others can be called in to help. London can never go short of water now, but this was not always the case; in fact it is only since the Metropolitan Water Board was set up in 1903 to manage the whole of London's water supplies that there has been sufficient. Before that year London was supplied by a number of independent water companies, and it was only in the area of the Kent Water Company, where the supply came from deep wells, that London could not go short of water in a dry season.

Let us go back to the beginning and see how it has all grown. The Romans always had a good water supply brought into their cities from natural or artificial lakes many miles away, but this was not necessary in Britain where there is plenty of rain all the year round, and so the houses in Roman London depended on their own wells just like the country cottages of to-day. Saxon London got its water in the same way and many of the wells are known by their Saxon names, such as Clerkenwell and St. Bride's Well; but as London filled up with houses these wells were not sufficient, and other means had to be found. Many of the houses near the Thames took their water from the river which was then a clear stream full of fish, and, as the tide was stopped by the narrow arches of London Bridge, which formed a dam, the water above bridge was fresh and not so muddy as it is to-day.

When people began to live in Cheapside and to the north they found that the wells were not so good and the river was a long way off; so, although men began to come round with water barrels on carts, a better supply had to be found. In the time of King John the citizens bought springs out in the country at Paddington and Notting Hill and dug canals to bring the water to a reservoir, the Bayswater Conduit near Tyburn, which is now the Marble Arch. From there the water was carried, in pipes made of the hollowed trunks of elm trees, along the Bayswater Road, Oxford Street and Holborn to Cheapside, where supply conduits were set up from which the citizens could get their water; on great days such as victory celebrations these could be arranged to supply wine instead of water. As everybody came to the conduits, they became recognized places for meeting friends or getting casual day labourers, and an amusing story is told of one of them where the chimney sweeps used to stand. A countryman, who had come up to London, had been passing along Cheapside and had seen the sweeps standing around the conduit. He wrote home to his wife : " I know now why London is such a wicked place. As I was going along the main street I saw the entrance to Hell and there were the Devil and his imps standing around it waiting to catch people and take them down." The wooden pipes were not very successful because it was easy for people on the route to bore holes in them and steal the water, and so in 1216, the merchants of Bruges paid for a leaden pipe of six inches bore to be laid down and those who wanted water had to pay for it.

Even King John, who wanted a supply for the Royal stables, situated where the National Gallery now stands, had to pay, and was only allowed a supply pipe of the bore of a goose-quill. These sources of supply were enough until the great growth of the city in Tudor times, when again they were found to be insufficient, and a Dutchman was allowed to fit a water-wheel at London Bridge for the purpose of raising water from the river. The wheel remained working until the eighteenth century when it was replaced by a Newcomen pump; but a further supply became necessary in the time of James I, and Sir Hugh Myddleton got permission to bring in water from springs in Hertfordshire and Middlesex. After spending all his own money and borrowing from the King and others he was successful, and his water-course, the New River, brought the water to a reservoir in Rosebery Avenue, where the head offices of the Metropolitan Water Board now stand. From the reservoir the water was carried to the conduits by means of elm pipes and people on the route were allowed to draw a supply for their houses on payment of an annual rent, for which they were permitted one supply pipe of lead

BATTERSEA POWER STATION

of an half-inch bore, the same size as the pipes in our houses.

Myddleton's New River, with supplies from the Thames and the village wells, proved sufficient until the early part of the nineteenth century, when London had grown so big that more water was necessary and a number of water companies were allowed to start work, each being given its own area to supply. Some of them got their water from the River Thames or the Lea and did not always trouble to filter it or get it free from disease germs. They sold the water to the better class houses, but the poorer people had to get theirs from standpipes in the streets, and as the water was only turned on for a few hours in the morning and not at all on Sundays there was always a good deal of trouble.

This was made worse whenever we had a dry summer, as the companies had no means of helping one another, and in dry seasons only the Kent Water Company, with its deep wells, had sufficient supplies. This led to the formation of the Metropolitan Water Board which took over all the companies in 1903 and was compelled to connect up the various systems and to supply every house with sufficient water for all household purposes in return for a water rate. The Board was allowed to charge extra for water used for gardens, for washing cars and for business purposes. So now we get a sufficient supply of water for which we either pay in our rent or by rates, and there is no fear of any part of London suffering from a drought.

What about those other pipes under the road ? The most important of them are the drains which carry off the sewage from our houses and the rain-water from our roofs and streets, a very important service in a place the size of London. Less than a century ago there was no real drainage outside the city and even there all the sewage ran into the Thames where it polluted the stream. The rain-water ran into the ditches as it does in the country to-day, and the house drains, when there were any, just discharged into a pit in the garden often next to the well. House rubbish was thrown out into the street or on to some waste bit of land and left there to breed flies and disease, with the result that there were terrible outbreaks of smallpox and other diseases. The Plague had stopped after the Great Fire, but smallpox, typhoid fever and cholera were frequent and many thousands died every year of these and other diseases. Something had to be done, especially when the smell became so bad at Westminster that the Members of Parliament were unable to go into the rooms facing the river. So in 1856 an Act of Parliament was passed setting up the Metropolitan Board of Works and giving it the duty of providing London with a proper drainage system. One of the first things the Board did was to construct two great main sewers, one on either side of the Thames, running from the west of the London area right down to Barking and Crossness, and to order that all local sewers should be connected with them. This got rid of the sewers that discharged into the Thames, although the storm water drains still connected with the river. Now every street has its sewer to which the house drains have to be connected in such a way that no sewage or gases can run back into the house, and each Borough Council has to connect these sewers with its main ones running deep under the roads. These in their turn are connected with the great main drains that are under the control of the L.C.C. which replaced the Board of Works in 1889. Besides giving London a good drainage system the Board of Works covered over the wide expanses of mud that were left at the sides of the river at low tide by building the three great embankments of London—the Victoria, the Albert and the Chelsea Embankments. The Board also made some fine new roads.

The great main sewers are huge tunnels, larger than those of the Underground railways; and, as so much of London is below the level of the tide, there have to be big pumping stations like those of the waterworks in order to keep the contents of the sewers moving. You can see one of these pumping stations near Chelsea Bridge. I expect you have seen the manhole covers to the sewers, those in the pavements leading to the smaller street sewers and those in the middle of the road to the larger main drains; and you may sometimes have seen the sewer men, with their high waterproof boots and their thick clothing, going down. The smaller sewers are inspected by means of square inspection chambers, but the larger ones are big enough for men to go along them and it is possible to walk for miles under London among these sewers. Let us take a short trip through one of the main sewers. Dressed in boots with tops that reach right up to our thighs, heavy woollen stockings, a heavy jacket and a waterproof hat, we will go down one of the manholes into the drain. When we get to the bottom we are in a tunnel rather larger than that of a tube railway, with a shallow stream of blackish water about six inches deep running at the bottom. It is quite warm down here, even in the winter ; but not too warm in summer, for the sewers are well ventilated, and there is practically no smell for the same reason. Here and there as we walk up the slope we see streams of water flowing in from smaller drains and we pass the iron ladders leading up to the manholes—very useful these if a sudden rush of air warns us that there has been a storm somewhere and that the water will rise many feet in a few minutes. There is nothing living in these sewers except an occasional rat which has escaped from a house drain, but there are not many of these for the men are down in the sewers every day and they kill all the rats they see, besides putting down poison. So we go on walking up-stream, past perhaps a stream of dirty, oily water from a garage or the pleasant smell from the discharge of a brewery or a scent works, until the tunnel gets too small for us to go any farther and we have to climb a ladder and come out into the street some miles away from where we started, none the worse for our adventure underground.

The other pipes underground are not nearly so exciting as these, and, except for the gas mains, they are all quite recent. Gas was first used in London in the early part of the nineteenth century, Piccadilly being the first street to be so lighted; but it took a long time for gas to come into general use. Now every street has its mains, usually one down each side, which join up to larger mains, and these to still larger ones running under the middle of the road in the main streets and so to the containers at or near the gas works where the gas is stored until it is wanted. Gas is supplied by the gas companies who have to fix and maintain all the mains and the service pipes, but the L.C.C. is responsible for testing the pressure and the heating quality and its inspectors also test the meters to see that they are working properly. Electricity is a newcomer, but there is now hardly a street that has not some kind of electric cable under it. The telegraph came first, then the telephone ; now there are cables carrying electric current as well, the service cables under the pavements and the mains in earthen-ware pipes very much like the drain pipes but very near the surface so that they can be got at easily. As a rule no hole has to be dug if anything goes wrong with any of these as there are inspection chambers along the streets and the cable can be drawn along to these and, if faulty, repaired and pulled back again.

Who is responsible for the lighting, cleaning and repair of our streets and roads ? Once this was the duty of every householder, who had to look after the pavement and road in front of his own house, but this system did not work very well even in the city. There, right down to the time of the Great Fire, people shot their rubbish and emptied their household waste water into the street, so that pedestrians had to keep close to the wall or they had their clothes spoiled. Here is a picture of the city streets in the middle of the eighteenth century taken from a poem called *Trivia*, written by John Gay, the author of *The Beggar's Opera*.

> Where a dim gleam the paly lantern throws
> O'er the mid pavement, heapy rubbish grows,
> Or arched vaults their gapy jaws extend,
> Or the dark caves to common shores extend,
> Oft by the wind the glimmering socket dies
> Ere night has half rolled round her ebon throne.

In the city, householders had to hang out a lantern with an inch of candle on moonless nights ; but else-where there was no sort of street lighting until 1762, when Westminster was lighted with oil-lamps. The use of these gradually spread, until by the early part of the nineteenth century most of the main roads and even

THE WATCH WITH "CRESSETS" AND
"BEACONS"
(Based on a print by Hollar)

some of the side streets were lighted, and the link-boy with his torch had quite disappeared. In those days the lamplighter was a very common sight. When the oil-lamps were in use he came round in the morning to fill and trim the lamps, then as it began to get dark he came round again, running up his ladder at each post to light the lamps. He had to go round in the night to relight any that had been blown out, and in the morning round he went again to put out the lights. He could still be seen in some parts early in this century going round with a long pole in the evening so that he could turn on the gas which was then lighted from a by-pass light. Now, except for cleaning or repair work, he has gone altogether, for the gaslights are controlled from a main stop-cock and the electric lights are worked from a switch. What a change there is too in the lighting of the streets. A hundred years ago the best lighting was about as bright as the starlights we had during the blackout; but now, with mercury vapour, yellow sodium or high-pressure gaslights slung over the middle of the road, the main roads are as light as day, and even in the side streets it is possible for us to see for more than a hundred yards ahead.

The care of our streets is now in the hands of the local Borough Council, whose Surveyor is responsible for all the work done on them. We have to pay for it out of the rates. In the city the Corporation has always looked after the streets and made rules for their care, but very few people took any notice of these rules until after the Great Fire, when the city authorities began to do the work themselves and to charge a rate for it. Outside the city even the main roads were like country lanes to-day, full of holes, dusty in the summer and muddy all the winter; whilst the side streets were no better than dirt tracks, although most of the Bloomsbury squares and some of the streets in the better part were paved and kept clean by the owners at the expense of their tenants. Then about a hundred years ago Paving and Lighting Boards were set up and they appointed surveyors whose duty it was to see that the pavements and roadways were properly made up and kept in repair. Sometimes a long street would have several of these Boards, each with its own ideas and so the street might have several different kinds of paving. There was one street in Westminster that had two Boards, one for each side of the road. Their territory met in the middle and as one believed in watering to lay the dust in the morning and the other thought the evening the best, the street was watered twice a day, but the dust was never laid.

A great change has come over our streets even in the last few years, and people who lived thirty years ago would hardly recognize them now. When practically every vehicle was drawn by horses whose hoofs pounded the road to dust, the water cart was very important during dry weather. The main roads were either covered by wood blocks or by granite sets, while the side streets were made up with granite chips or flints rolled well in. If it were kept in repair, this made an excellent surface for horse traffic, but, as the motor tyres wore it out, something else had to be found. Many

G

surfaces were tried but nothing has been found so good as cement laid down on a strong wire netting over a foundation of concrete, and so most of our roads are now made in this way, with the surface either tar sprayed every summer or covered with pitch to keep out the rain which would get down through the cracks and rot the foundation.

We have gone a very long way from our hole in the road; so let us get back and see what has happened. The men who dug this hole were working for the Water Board, but they might have been the workmen of any authority that has pipes under the road, or even the workmen of a builder who was putting up a house and had to open the road because of the work they were doing. But you cannot rope off a bit of road and dig a hole just as you like. First the Borough Surveyor has to be told because he will want to have a look in your hole and he will also want to see that it is filled in properly; probably his own men will come along and finish the job after your workmen have put back and rammed hard all the stuff they took out. Then you have to tell the police, for traffic might have to be stopped, and that is their work. Just as the local Council, through its Surveyor, is responsible for the upkeep of the road, so the police are responsible for seeing that it is properly used, and that too is a job they do for the people who live in the road; they are the ones who are really responsible. At first every householder was his own policeman and the people had to form parties to go on watch every night just as the street fire-parties did during the War. Now you know that some of these fire-parties did their work very well but others were a bit slack, and so the Government had to make rules about it and fire-watching became compulsory. Just the same sort of thing happened about the policing of the streets: in some it was done well, in others badly, and at last rules had to be made. It was then found that the compulsory police duties interfered with work, and so a constable was appointed in each parish who had to arrange for the watch to be properly manned. In the city, where the alderman of each ward was responsible, the watch was generally pretty good, but outside the city area the men appointed were usually elderly cripples, chosen because they were cheap. Each carried an halberd which he was much too weak to use and had a lantern and a rattle to give warning of his approach. So that he might sleep in peace, he had a kind of sentry box and the street gangs used to make sure that the watch would not interfere with them by quietly tipping up the box over the sleeping man and leaving him there for the constable to find on his rounds.

Some improvement was made when the Bow Street magistrates formed a special force of their own, whose duty was to guard the district for which these magistrates were responsible, and a body of officers, the Bow Street Runners, was formed and given the task of tracking down criminals and bringing them to justice. These runners were so effective that in 1829 Sir Robert Peel set up a new force for the whole of the London area, the Metropolitan Police, and their blue uniform soon became a familiar sight in the streets. At first they were dressed like the gentlemen of the time in blue frock coats, tight trousers and tall hats, but after a while they were put into their present style of uniform which has been copied by every police force in the country. They were usually called either Bobbies or Peelers, after the name of their founder, and they are still controlled by the Home Secretary and not by the London County Council. The City of London, however, managed to keep its own police force, and so to-day, when you go into the city you will notice that the police uniforms are slightly different from those of the rest of London. The two forces work together very well, but this is just one of the many things in which the city has managed to keep control of its own affairs.

Our hole in the road has now shown us what a lot of people are concerned with the making and upkeep of our roads.   First of all there are the people who live in the road.   It is their road, and they are the ones who are really responsible for looking after it and seeing that other people use it properly.   In past ages they were supposed to do this work themselves, but it was often a very tiresome duty and many of them were too busy to do the work themselves and could not afford to pay men to do it for them.   When roads became very busy and the traffic was so heavy that the road surface required special work, the householder was unable to do the work himself, and so he had to pay special people to do it for him.   For a long time roads were controlled by special bodies of people, the Road Commissioners, who looked after the road and charged the cost to the inhabitants as a rate or to the users by means of tolls.   Even to-day the householder is the first person responsible for a road, and when a new street is built the owners of the houses have to see that the road is properly made up before the local Council will take it over.   Sometimes this work is done by the builder or by a road contractor whom he employs ; sometimes the local Council will do it; but always the cost is charged to the owners.   When the road has been taken over it is the local authority which looks after it. In London this is generally the Borough Council, but nevertheless the inhabitants have to pay.

Sometimes the street lighting is installed and maintained by the gas or electricity company that supplies the district and the Council then pays them out of the rates.   Sometimes the Council itself supplies the lighting, either buying the current or gas, or, if it has a power station of its own, supplying the current itself, but again the people have to pay.   Gas and electricity companies, the Post Office, the water supplier and sometimes other people too have pipes under the road and they have to keep them in order and make good any damage they may do.   Then the police are responsible for the control of traffic and of those who use the road, though the local Council has to provide the traffic lights and the

crossing controls.   The Borough Council too is responsible for the local drains whilst the County Council
provides the great main drains.

There are other bodies, however, who have a say in
the control and maintenance of roads, looking after the
great main routes that are of more than local importance.
Main roads and the bridges on their routes are usually
looked after by the County Council, though the local
Borough Councils generally take care of their upkeep
within their own boroughs.   Widening and straighten-
ing of these main roads, building new bridges to carry
them over rivers, and other work of this kind is generally
done by the London County Council, which also looks
after the bridges and tunnels that form the crossing of the
Thames, except for those within the City of London
which are looked after by the City Corporation.

Then there are the great arterial roads that run through
London to other parts of the country.   These are the
concern of the Ministry of Transport, acting under the
authority of Parliament, for these roads are a national
concern.   Outside London the Ministry often builds
these roads, leaving the County Council to keep them
in repair, but in London the actual work is usually done
by the London County Council, the Ministry providing
part of the cost out of national funds.

You must remember, however, that, whoever does
the work, it is the people themselves who are really
responsible for it, just as they are for every other piece
of control, whether it is keeping their street clean or
deciding what shall be done about foreign affairs.

CHAPTER VI

LONDON'S MARKETS

HAVE you ever considered how London is fed; how all the millions of Londoners get their clothes, their shoes and all the things they need; or thought of the thousands of railway trains, road lorries and ships coming into London with all the goods needed by so many people? Have you ever asked yourself how all these things get into the shops where they are sold; or thought of the great wholesale stores where the reserves are kept so that the shops are never short? Most of you will have seen one of those fascinating street markets that may be found in many parts of London; but have you been to Covent Garden Market in the early morning to see the fruit and flowers; and have you seen the meat and poultry at Smithfield, the fish at Billingsgate, the potatoes and vegetables at the Borough Market, or the live cattle in their thousands at the Caledonian Market in Islington? If you have, you will have seen something very interesting and you will have some idea of how London is fed and clothed. For London grows very little of its own food and none of the wool and silk and cotton for its clothes. All its fish and its meat, its bread and its milk, its leather and its cloth have to come to it from outside, and a wonderful organization for supplying all these things has been built up through many centuries. Here are nearly ten millions of people who must be fed and clothed by the work of others. Farmers in Britain and many other parts of the world, sheep-masters in Australia, cotton growers in the United States of America, fruit growers in all parts of the world, all help to supply London. All their produce has to be brought by rail, road or sea in large quantities, and then sold in smaller lots to the shops, where it is sold to us. This work is done by the organization of markets.

COVENT GARDEN MARKET

As we have already seen, London began as a trading centre, and almost from the beginning the farmers from the country brought their spare produce for sale in its markets, although the markets of Roman London dealt mostly in slaves, metals, timber, corn and other produce of the country, and the manufactured goods that came in from Europe. Saxon London was the same, although probably it was more like the market of a country town to-day; but gradually trade grew, and more people came to live in London. They were too busy to grow their own food and markets had to be organized so that they could be fed and clothed.

In the Middle Ages markets and fairs were the only places where goods could be bought and sold. The farmer with anything to spare took it to market, so did the weaver, the metal worker and other craftsmen. Here they met buyers, and goods could be exchanged, or materials like wool collected into large quantities for shipment abroad. The only difference between a fair and a market was that the fair was held only at fixed times in the year, usually once, and lasted for several days, whilst the market was held regularly each week or even daily. In either case the fair or market was very much like those you can see to-day in country towns or in a London street, with temporary stalls set up in the road, in some open space outside the town gate, or by a monastery or castle where there was someone powerful enough to keep order and to see that trading was done fairly. In England all market rights belonged to the King, and included police duties, the fixing of prices and the punishment of offenders in the Piepowder Court (so-called from the Old French *pied poudré*, meaning " dusty feet "). You will see the reason for the name if you will think of all the people at the market who had walked miles along the dusty roads to get there. Holding a market was a profitable thing, for dues were paid on all goods sold, and the stall-holders usually paid a small rent too. It was almost impossible for the King to manage all markets, and so he usually let or sold the rights to some town or lord, and the markets in London, and for seven miles around, were controlled by the City Corporation. This made it difficult for markets to be held anywhere except in or just outside the city itself. The citizens wanted the profits for their own use, so most of the London markets were kept within the walls. Even to-day the City Corporation is the most important market authority for the London area.

Market prices in those days were always carefully fixed by the market authority. Those who tried to keep goods out of the market by buying them up before they got in, or who tried to force up the prices (forestallers and regrators they were called), were severely punished, generally by being put in the pillory at the market so that everyone should know what they had been doing—an excellent punishment which might well be revived to-day, especially for those who try to buy up large quantities of foodstuffs and so force up the prices.

The whole of medieval London was really one great market, but the most important centre was along Cheapside and in Cannon Street and Eastchepe. Here there were shops on both sides of the street and a double row of stalls set back-to-back along the middle of the road. Each kind of goods was sold in one part of the town, and the names of many of the city streets to-day remind us of the things that used to be sold there. At the west end of Chepe, besides the shops of the goldsmiths, there were shops and stalls for selling food. About the middle, near where the Mansion House stands, was the Stocks Market for meat and dried fish. In the Poultry, fowls and game were sold, and in Eastchepe was another food market, mostly for cooked food. Fish were landed at Billingsgate and sold in Fish Street. Oranges, lemons and dried fruits from the Mediterranean countries were landed at Botolph's Wharf and sold in the parish of

St. Clement, Eastchepe.   Secondhand clothes were sold
in the streets around Aldgate as they are to-day.

There is an old poem called *London Lykpenny* which
gives a very interesting picture of all these markets.   It
tells of a countryman who had come up to London on
some business but found when he got there that he
could not do much because of the way his money melted
away.   London fairly licked it up ; and the poor man had
to go back hungry and disappointed in spite of all the
good things that were for sale.

> Then to the Chepe I gan me drawn
> Where much people I saw for to stand,
> One offered me velvet, silk and lawn ;
> Another he taketh me by the hand,
> Here is Paris thread the finest in the land.
>
> .   .   .   .
>
> Then when I forth by London Stone
> Throughout all the Canwyk (Cannon) Street,
> Drapers much cloth offered me anon.
> Then comes one who cried, " Hot sheep's feet,"
> One cried " Mackerel," " Rushes green " another
> Gan me greet.

But he could not afford to buy anything because all his
money but twopence was already spent and, to make
matters worse, when he got into the secondhand clothes
section he was offered his own hood, which had been
stolen in Cheapside.   You can almost see the crowded
street and the jostling people, and hear the cries of the
stall-holders.

The fairs, too, were very interesting.   In and around
Smithfield there was an important cattle and horse fair
that drew buyers from all parts of Europe, whilst only
a few yards away was Bartholomew Fair, held in front
of the hospital and monastery and controlled by the
monks of St. Bartholomew's Priory.   The profits of this
fair went to the upkeep of the hospital.   It became
purely a pleasure fair, but one part of it, the Cloth Fair,

was permanent, and the name still survives in a street which contained many of the old houses until a few years ago, when they were pulled down. There was a fair held at Westminster for the benefit of the leper hospital of St. James, which has given its name to the district of Mayfair ; whilst at Southwark and in Bermondsey there were others. There were two hay-markets : one in Westminster in the street of that name, and the other in Whitechapel High Street. Greenwich, Camberwell, Hampstead and many of the other villages now included in London also had their fairs. Those of Greenwich and Hampstead have survived as Bank Holiday pleasure fairs, but all the others have been closed or have changed to street markets.

Of the modern markets one of the most interesting is Covent Garden, the great flower, fruit and vegetable market just off Drury Lane. Once this was really a garden—the kitchen garden of the monks of Westminster, and perhaps, like so many kitchen gardeners, they used to sell their surplus produce at the garden gate. All we know for certain is that in the time of Charles I the garden became the property of the Earl of Bedford, who made it into a square with houses round and a piazza or covered walk in front of the houses. Here the country people came with their vegetables to sell them to the cooks from the great houses in Drury Lane and the neighbourhood, then the fashionable district ; and it was out of this irregular street market that the great Covent Garden Market grew. Later the Earl had sheds built for the stall-holders, and later still the place passed to a company who set up the present market. Although within the seven miles radius to which the market authority of the City Corporation extends, Covent Garden is still the property of a company to whom all the stall-holders pay rent. It is a wonderful sight to go into the flower market early in the morning, especially about Easter when the Spring flowers are in, or in June when the whole place is full of roses. The fruit market is also very interesting and full of colour, especially during the orange season. Perhaps the most remarkable sight is the market porters each balancing a high tower of round baskets on his head.

The other great vegetable market is in the Borough, just behind Southwark Cathedral and half hidden under the arches of the railway. This began as a street market in the Borough High Street, but it was found to interfere with the traffic over London Bridge and so in the middle of the eighteenth century it was removed to its present position. This market is managed by trustees, some of whom are appointed by the Cathedral authorities and some by the people of Southwark.

The market for the city itself is at Leadenhall, right on the site of the market place of Roman London. As fruit and vegetables were sold here in the Middle Ages, Leadenhall Market has probably been continuous since Roman times and has always been owned by the city. In the fourteenth century it was ordered that all poultry for sale in the city should be sold here; in the seventeenth century it became a meat market; and it is now a general provision market with a section selling flowers, fruit and vegetables. It also has a retail section.

Another fruit and vegetable market is at Spitalfields. Here there was a street market which the Corporation took over at the beginning of this century and made into a wholesale market for supplying the East End of London. Besides these, there are markets at Greenwich and in several of the outer boroughs. These markets supply the more remote parts of London, whilst at Bromley, Croydon and Waltham Abbey there are real country markets although these places are now joined to London.

London consumes an enormous amount of meat, and so its meat markets are very important. There are now two, both under the control of the Corporation; but until the First World War there was a third, the Foreign Cattle Market at Deptford where live cattle were brought in from America and killed. Improvements in refrigeration have made it possible to bring meat from the Argentine and Australasia, too far away for the animals to be brought alive. At the same time the supplies from North America fell off, and so the Deptford market was closed. The only two meat markets left are Smithfield, where dead meat is sold, and the Caledonian Market at Islington for live cattle. Smithfield was an important cattle market in the Middle Ages and it continued to be the most important live-cattle market for London until about a hundred years ago. Then the Corporation built a market for dead meat, the largest in London and one of the biggest in the world. There are, in fact, two markets, one under the other, for underground there are huge cold stores and a great railway station. This railway has direct communication with the docks so that the meat can be put on to insulated vans from the ships and run straight in to the cold stores at the market. In these stores there are many miles of overhead tramway lines for carrying the sides of beef and carcases of sheep, and there is space for thousands of tons of meat.

The Caledonian Market is for live cattle and sheep and takes the place of the market that used to be at Smithfield. A hundred years ago the cattle and sheep used to walk to London, grazing as they came; some from Scotland, others from Wales or the North, and many from the Home Counties. Just before Christmas great flocks of geese and turkeys came from Norfolk. They too had walked, starting as soon as the harvest was over and grazing over the stubbles as they came. To protect their feet they were tarred and sanded and it must have been a wonderful sight to see thousands of birds arriving at the markets, which were then at Smithfield. Now the birds are killed and plucked on the farms and are brought in by special railway refrigerator vans. Besides the cattle market which is held on Tuesdays and Fridays there is a general market on Mondays and Thursdays. Here anything can be bought : dogs, songbirds (some of these, alas, turn out to be only painted

CALEDONIAN MARKET

sparrows), clothes both new and secondhand, books, pictures, wireless sets, spare parts for machinery—anything and everything may be bought here. Sometimes wonderful bargains are reported but the dealers usually

know the value of the things they sell and it is generally
they who make the bargains.

London's other big market is at Spitalfields. This
used to be a fair held in front of the leper hospital of
St. Mary and the actual market started there at the end
of the seventeenth century, long after the hospital disappeared. At the beginning of the present century the
City Corporation bought all the market rights, put up
buildings and made a compact and an up-to-date market
in place of the old straggling lines of stalls that used to
line the road.

The old rhyme,

> Oranges and Lemons
> Say the bells of St. Clements,

reminds us that, in the Middle Ages, fruits from the
countries of the Mediterranean Sea used to be landed
at Botolph's Wharf in the parish of St. Clement, Eastchepe, and sold in the streets around. To-day one may
still see the fruit boats unloading at the same place and
long lines of men straggling up the gang-planks with
boxes of oranges. Now, the oranges go to Covent
Garden market to be sold, and as this market is near to
the parish of St. Clement Danes, some books will tell
you that this is the church of the rhyme. I do not think
it is because the rhyme is very much older than Covent
Garden Market, and St. Clement Danes was out in the
country in the Middle Ages. Besides, all the bells taking
part in the conversation are those of city churches, and
the great bell of St. Mary-le-Bow settles the argument;
so I think we must dismiss the claim of St. Clement
Danes and keep the rhyme to the city where it belongs.

Along the Bermondsey bank of the river the provision
boats unload butter, eggs, bacon and cheese to be stored
in the warehouses of Tooley Street, many of them in
the arches of the railway viaduct. There is generally
a great crowd of people along the downstream side of
London Bridge watching all the boats moving about,

the men unloading them, and the foreign sailors on their decks, just as I expect the Londoners of past ages used to watch the great galleys of Venice and Florence unloading all the strange things they had brought to the same landing places and wharves.

Bread is our other great food. It comes, either as flour or grain, from abroad, for there is not nearly enough English corn grown. In former times when the corn was mostly English, the flour came straight to the London bakers from the country millers, but the Corporation had also to buy and store large quantities of grain which they held in case of scarcity. Then when prices rose and the poor could not afford to buy bread, the city corn was put on the market, or sold to the bakers who were compelled to sell to the poor at a low price the bread they made from it. Sometimes it was given away to the poor. To pay for this corn the Corporation was allowed to tax the corn sold in the ordinary way, and there is still a Coal and Corn Committee of the Corporation although it does not deal either in coal or corn to-day. The Corporation mills were at London Bridge and were driven by the power of the waterfall that we spoke of in the chapter on the bridge. The tax has now been abolished, together with that on coal, so the Committee now acts as the Finance Committee of the Corporation, but it still manages the Coal Exchange. There is a Corn Exchange in Mark Lane, which is the private property of the wholesale corn merchants. Here the corn used to be sold by the sack and buyers were allowed to take samples from the sacks to examine. These samples were then thrown on the floor and there was a great deal of waste, but to-day things are different. Most of the corn comes in from overseas and is landed and stored in the docks. Standard samples are taken from each consignment and sent to the Exchange, and the purchasers buy on these, so that to-day there is hardly any waste.

Another product sold by sample is coal, and this market, unlike that for corn, is controlled by the Corporation although it has nothing to do with the actual sales, which are managed by representatives of the great London coal merchants who meet the colliery representatives at the Exchange. Coal was first brought to London by sea in the reign of Henry III, and the London merchants who sold the coal by retail used to meet the captains of the collier boats, who represented the owners of the mines, in the taverns near Billingsgate, off which the ships were anchored. For many centuries there was a tax on imported coal, but the Corporation was allowed to bring in a certain amount free of duty and to hold it for distribution to the poor. When London was burned by the Great Fire the Corporation was allowed to use the proceeds of the Coal Tax for rebuilding St. Paul's Cathedral and some of the city churches and other public buildings, and so by a kind of poetic justice the mineral that gives us most of our fuel was made to pay part of the cost of our greatest fire. The first Coal Exchange was a private affair like the Corn Exchange to-day, but at the beginning of the nineteenth century the Corporation bought the rights and built a market at the corner of Thames Street and St. Mary at Hill, just opposite to Billingsgate. Here in 1849 the present building was erected. The market is held in a high-domed room with a floor made of pieces of many woods in the pattern of a mariner's compass, the indicator being an anchor of black oak from a tree that was found in the bed of the River Tyne, the shank of the anchor pointing to the north. At one time there was a tell-tale wind vane in the roof of the dome so that the merchants could see which way the wind was blowing. If it were west the collier brigs were held up at Blackwall and coal was scarce so that prices were high ; but if the wind changed to the east the boats got in together and prices fell rapidly. Another very interesting thing to be seen here is the Roman heating chamber, probably the hot room of a bath. It is right under the present building and is reached by an iron staircase from one of the

H

entrance passages. The original floor has gone, so that
the actual arrangement of the flues by which it was
heated can be seen quite easily.

London has many other markets besides those we
have already described. Some are for foods and some
for raw materials, and the actual markets are held either
at the docks or at offices in Mincing Lane and its neighbourhood; but for a few articles there are market buildings, all, however, owned and managed by the merchants
who deal in the various goods. There is a Metal
Exchange where there are dealings in metals other than
iron, a Baltic Exchange where timber and other things
that come mainly from the countries of the Baltic Sea
are dealt in, and a number of others.

One of the most important of London's other wholesale markets is the Wool Exchange. Wool has always
been an important item in London's trade, and in the
sixteenth century, after the French captured Calais
where the great wool market had been, London became
the centre of the wool trade not only for England but for
the whole of Western Europe. The sales were private
until Australian wool began to come to Britain in large
quantities, when public sales were held. To-day wool
sales are held in the Wool Exchange in Coleman Street
six times a year. The wool comes in to the docks where
it is sorted and graded by the officials of the Port of
London Authority. The buyers see the wool at the
docks, mark their catalogues, and the wool is then sold
by catalogue numbers at auctions held in the Exchange.
The wool sold and the merchants who buy come from
all parts of the world and the prices obtained fix the
world price of wool, even for wools that never come anywhere near London.

Tea, spices and many other materials are dealt with
by merchants who have their offices in or near Mincing
Lane, the buyers going round and seeing or tasting
samples. The P.L.A. has set up other markets in its
warehouses at the docks. Producers send their goods

here from all parts of the world, the P.L.A. grades and catalogues them and holds auction or private sales at certain times. In this way London has become the world market for many things besides those actually used there.

The street market is a typical London sight and is probably as old as London itself. Except that the goods are displayed on stalls, these street markets are not like the country markets to which the farmers bring their produce. Street markets usually begin quite by accident. Some costermongers find that a particular street makes a good stand, and, when they are not moved on by the police, they get into the habit of standing there, and so a market grows up. Many of these markets are of recent origin but some of them are quite old. They sell chiefly flowers, fruit, and food of various kinds ; but sometimes other things are sold as well ; and there are one or two where very little food is sold. One of the most interesting of these is the clothes market in Petticoat Lane, or Middlesex Street as it should be called. This market had been settled in Eastchepe and the neighbourhood for a very long time, and it was here that the poor countryman of the *London Lykpenny* was offered his own hood. To-day the market is held just outside the city, not only in Middlesex Street but in many other streets in the district. Here can be bought anything in clothing : misfits from the great West End tailors, new goods especially made in the East End for this market, cast off clothes from Mayfair, and clothes that have already been worn by more than one owner. The scene on a Sunday morning is a very animated one, for the people are mostly foreigners, and the shouting, gesticulating crowd seems to be speaking all the languages on earth. One is surrounded by clothes : clothes on stalls and barrows, clothes in shops and outside shops, clothes strung on lines across the street, and clothes hanging out of the upper windows and on poles above the shops, clothes of every possible shape, size and colour, even clothes draped on the arms and round the shoulders of sellers who have no stall or barrow—a scene more like an eastern bazaar than a London market.

In Leather Lane and the neighbourhood there is another foreign market, Italian this time; whilst not far away, in Farringdon Road, is one where the chief things for sale are old books, plants and flowers, seeds, spares for all kinds of machinery and junk of all sorts. In Soho there is yet another foreign market, Levantine, in Greek Street; but in the neighbouring Berwick Street the shops, stall-holders and buyers are nearly all French and the market looks like that of a French country town.

Another, but typically English market, is in the High Street, Lambeth, extending into Lambeth Walk and right along through the Lower Marsh and the New Cut to Waterloo Road. There is another in East Lane, Walworth. Every part of London has its street markets, each different from the others, but all alike in many ways and very useful in supplying the poorer parts of London with cheap food and other things. In some of the outer suburbs and the country towns like Croydon, Bromley or Waltham Abbey there are real country markets, sometimes for selling cattle or other farm produce, sometimes a sort of Saturday mixture of the London street market and the regular country market; but these are hardly London markets although the places where they are held are now joined to London by continuous streets of houses.

CHAPTER VII

HEALTH OF BODY AND MIND

IN a place so large as London it is very important that bodies and minds shall be kept healthy, and so we must have plenty of hospitals and schools of various kinds, not only to keep us healthy but as places where the best ways of doing this may be studied. At first both schools and hospitals were managed entirely by the Church, although quite early in the Middle Ages the city companies, and later the Corporation itself had schools. To-day our schools and hospitals are managed not by the Church, but either by private committees who collect the necessary money by private subscriptions, or by the London County Council; and, for some purposes, by the local Borough Council, which collects money from all of us through the rates. The great London hospitals too are schools where doctors and nurses are trained. At the head of the whole system is the University of London.

Let us think first of the hospitals. A great London hospital, whether managed by the L.C.C. or by a private Board of Governors, is a wonderful place. If you have ever been into one, either as a patient or to see friends who are patients, you will have seen something of its working; but the patients and their friends see only a small part of what really goes on. They meet the nurses and the doctors, they see the students coming round to study, but they never see the most wonderful part of all—the laboratories, the offices and the kitchens, the lecture-rooms and the libraries where the doctors and nurses are trained. Even the patients see very little of the work that goes on in all these parts of the hospital. They never meet the pathologists and the bacteriologists who work in the laboratories, studying the diseases and trying to find new cures. They never think of the great army of people whose work is carried on outside the wards, the plumbers and carpenters who look after the buildings, the electricians who see that the lighting and power are always ready, the furnace men who keep the heat going, the laundresses and sewing maids who look after the linen, or the gardeners who keep the outside grounds neat and orderly.   Behind all these there are the Medical Superintendent and the Matron, the Secretary and the office staff, and behind these again the Board of Governors of a voluntary hospital or the Hospitals Committee of the L.C.C., to see that everything is managed in the best way.   Then there is the Ministry of Health which links up all the various health services of the country into one great whole.

Not all health work is done in the hospitals.   There are the out-patients' departments and dispensaries where people can go for treatment if they are not so ill that they have to be in hospital ; there are the doctors who see private patients or to whom you go if you are a panel patient ; and there are the Medical Officers of Health who have to do what they can to prevent illness by looking after drains and water supply, seeing that houses are kept in good condition, and stopping the spread of infectious diseases.   Nor must we forget the School Medical Service with its doctors, dentists and nurses who have to see that children and young people of school age are properly nourished and kept healthy.

The oldest of all the London hospitals is St. Bartholomew's in Smithfield, founded by Rahere, the Court Jester to Henry II, in 1123.   Rahere had gone on a pilgrimage to Rome and whilst there he fell ill.   During his illness he thought he was hovering over a deep pit, and just as he was about to fall into it, he saw St. Bartholomew who offered to save him if he would promise to build a hospital when he returned to London.   This Rahere did, choosing a dreary marsh at Smithfield as the place where he would build.   He began by building a monastery church, the choir of which still exists as the church of

THE SUN BALCONY AT MILE END HOSPITAL

St. Bartholomew the Great; and just opposite he built his hospital so that it could be managed by the monks. It continued in its monastic form until the reign of Henry VIII, when all the monasteries were dissolved. The monastic buildings were destroyed, but the citizens bought the hospital and in 1544 it was refounded by Sir Thomas Gresham. Soon afterwards a medical school was founded, so that " Bart's " is not only the oldest hospital in London but has the oldest medical school. The hospital survived the Great Fire, but it has recently been rebuilt; the only really old parts left are the gateway and the chapel.

The second oldest hospital is that of St. Thomas's, which was founded by the monks of St. Mary's Priory (their church is now Southwark Cathedral down by London Bridge) in the thirteenth century. The hospital used to stand on the site of London Bridge Station, and like St. Bart's, it was bought by the citizens and refounded as an ordinary hospital. The hospital of those days would have seemed a queer place to us, for the wards were dark and narrow; there were no doctors or surgeons on the staff of the hospital until 1566 and both patients and nurses were whipped if they were disobedient. The patients all had to go to church on Sunday mornings or they got no dinner; and those who were too ill to eat the ordinary food were given a quart of ale instead of their food.

Guy's Hospital, just across the road from the old St. Thomas's, was founded by Thomas Guy, a rather miserly bookseller, in 1721. At first the two hospitals worked almost as one, even sharing the skeleton from which the students of both learned how the human bones were put together. But when the railway came, St. Thomas's sold their site and building to the railway company, and with the money built a new hospital opposite the Houses of Parliament. During the nineteenth century when London was growing rapidly, many new hospitals were founded, some in connection with the Colleges of the University, some for the treatment of special diseases, and some in the very poor parts where people could not afford to go to doctors. To-day London has a great many of these hospitals—the voluntary hospitals we call them because they get their money from private subscriptions and from collections in churches and in the streets. But there were never enough of these hospitals, especially for the very poor; so the Boards of Guardians, who during the nineteenth century had to care for the poor, began to build hospitals where these people could be looked after. In 1932 these were all taken over by the L.C.C. which has now set up a fine system of public hospitals paid for out of the rates. At first many people did not like these. They thought they were an inferior kind of hospital, but this prejudice is rapidly disappearing and the two kinds of hospital, the voluntary and the public, work together for the health of the Londoner.

When most of our hospitals were built, London was a fairly quiet place and the buildings were generally away from the most noisy streets ; but during the last twenty years this has altered, and now, by the growth of London, many of them find they are right on the noisy main roads. Moreover, when they were first built no one thought that one of the best cures for most illnesses was air and sunlight, so that the older hospital wards were dark and dreary places, very different from the light and airy wards of a modern hospital. Most of the London hospitals were thinking of rebuilding when the " blitz " came and they had to remove their patients out into the country. This removal has shown them that all but the most seriously ill can be moved with safety, and so it seems very likely that they will now build new hospitals outside London where patients can get plenty of light and air, and keep their old buildings for out-patients, and as clearing stations where patients can be taken for emergency treatment and moved out to the main hospital as soon as possible.

Education is another matter that the Londoner has to think about. A healthy body is of very little use unless it is guided by a healthy mind, and education means a lot more than just going to school whilst you are a child. We must learn to read and write before we can really begin to learn anything, because to-day our information comes to us mainly from books ; so when we have learned to read we are just ready to begin our real studies. Like the work of healing the sick, education was once carried on almost entirely by the Church. Most parish clergymen had a little school in a room over the church porch where they taught reading and writing as well as some special church teaching, and from these schools promising boys and girls were sent on to the monastic schools. In medieval London there were plenty of schools of all kinds, little parish schools, monastic schools belonging to the great abbeys, the cathedral school at St. Pauls, and the Guild schools where the apprentices were taught whatever book work was necessary for them in their trade. There was the apprenticeship itself, too, by which the boy not only learned a trade but had a practical training in citizenship as well, so that by the time he became a master he knew a great deal of what was going on in the world and was well able to make up his own mind from practical experience on many matters for which we to-day have to depend entirely on our newspapers.

When the monastery schools were closed at the Reformation their places were taken by the Grammar Schools and the Charity Schools of which there were many in and around London. The most important of these were St. Paul's School, refounded by Dean Colet in 1510; St. Peter's School, Westminster, a continuation of the old Abbey School; Christ's Hospital, founded in 1553 as a home for London orphans; the Charterhouse, founded in the reign of James I by Thomas Sutton; and the new school of "God's Gift" founded at Dulwich by Shakespeare's friend, the actor Edward Alleyn. Besides these there were the Mercer's and other guild schools and a number of schools in the villages round London, and in these the children were taught until they were old enough to be apprenticed. But in places like St. Giles-in-the-Fields, where there were slums, the children did not go to school at all: they just ran wild, learned to steal at an early age, and sometimes ended by being transported or hanged at Tyburn.

In the eighteenth century the Industrial Revolution began and destroyed very much of the old English life. The children were wanted in the mills and the factories where they could earn money as soon as they were able to walk, and a great new class sprang up whose members had never been to school, a class which soon became the most numerous in the country. The tradespeople and the better-class artisans, however, wanted their children to have a little book-learning, and so private schools sprang up. Working mothers wanted their children minded and small schools were started in the factory districts. The

Wesleyan movement wakened the consciences of church people who began to teach the Christian faith to what was practically a heathen people and found that they would have to teach reading and writing first, or it would be impossible to teach anything to such large numbers. So school education began again for the ordinary people. Here is a picture of one of those early schools taken from a Government report published in 1838, when people were fearing a revolution and were beginning to discover how the working people lived. If you compare it with your own schools you will see how great has been the improvement within the last hundred years.

In a garret up three pair of stairs was a common day school in a room measuring ten feet by nine. On a perch forming a triangle with a corner of the room was a cock and two hens, under a stump bed in the corner was a dog-kennel in the occupation of three black terriers, whose barking, added to the voices of the children and the cackling of the hens, was almost deafening. There was only one small window at which sat the master, obscuring what light there was.

At about the same time as this school existed, Church schools were being built, little two-roomed buildings in the churchyard where the master taught with the help of the elder children and with a young mistress in charge of the infants. There are a few of these little schools still to be found in London, usually with a few more rooms added or the big room divided up. In the country districts, however, they are very common, exactly as they were a century ago ; and some of you may actually have been taught in one of them during the evacuation period.

This sort of thing went on until 1870, when the Government decided that there should be a school place for every child whose parents wanted it to go to school and School Boards were set up in London and throughout the country. They were to build schools wherever necessary, paying for them out of the rates, and the London School Board soon began to build schools all over London : big schools with several classrooms and a teacher to each class besides the master in charge of the whole school. The classes were very large, with sixty or seventy pupils in the lower part of the school, and the teaching was very different from that of to-day. The children in such big classes had to be drilled rather than taught : they had to learn to sit still all day with their arms folded unless they were writing or drawing, and every child in the class had to be doing the same thing at the same time. There was no splitting the class up into little groups each doing its own work ; none of that free movement about the room to which you are accustomed ; no craft, science or domestic rooms ; no gym and no art-room, although most of these were being introduced by the time your parents were at school. The School Board was allowed to have only elementary schools. It was not allowed to teach foreign languages or science or any other more advanced work, and it was not allowed to have secondary or technical schools. So in 1905 it was abolished and all London education placed under the L.C.C. which was already responsible for higher education. Now that all kinds of education were controlled by one authority it was possible to fit each into a scheme so that children could pass easily from one sort of school to another by means of scholarships. Since 1918 many other changes have been made. Not only have the ordinary schools been improved and fitted up with craft rooms and halls, but Senior and Central schools have been built with science, art and practical work-rooms suitable for the older boys and girls. There are more scholarships to the secondary schools ; and there are technical schools where boys and girls may learn a trade. It has been made easy for them to learn outside the school building by going to museums, art galleries and famous buildings, by working in libraries and even by wandering about in London itself, visiting the streets and the factories, the docks and the river, learning in the best of all ways by seeing what is going on. We are beginning to get back something of that practical training in citizenship which the boy in the Middle Ages received whilst he was an apprentice.

But education is not entirely a matter of sitting at a desk in a school or even in a college ; even book-learning does not stop when one leaves school, and so the Londoner now has plenty of opportunities for further education. For those older boys and girls who want to become more skilled in their trade there are the Evening Institutes and Young Peoples' Colleges, commercial or technical ; and for those older people who want to learn for pleasure rather than to become more skilled there are the Literary and other adult Institutes and all sorts of lectures and discussion classes open to all who wish to attend.

Most of you will have seen your Public Library. Probably you borrow story books from it, but have you ever thought of it as a place where you can learn ? Yet a library is such a place ; in fact those of us who studied at a University did most of our work in the library. Most of the history written in this book was learned by working in libraries, either in those of the London boroughs or in one of the big central libraries, so that you can see how important these places are. Your own local library has in it a lot more than just story books, and your librarian will be only too pleased to advise you if you want to borrow books on any special subject. He will even get them for you if they are not in his own library. Your local library, too, is the best place from which to start if you want to learn anything about the history of your own district, and all the London districts have histories that are very interesting. The library usually has all the books that have been written about the borough and there is often a collection of pictures that will show you how the district has changed even in the last few years. So use your library for much more than borrowing story books.

Besides the schools, colleges and libraries, there are the museums and picture galleries. These are not just dull places where one may spend a wet Saturday afternoon if one has not enough money to go to the cinema. They are places where a very interesting story is being told in the most fascinating way, not from books but from the things made by man. Most of them are far too crowded with exhibits, but then you need not look at everything at once; and in most of our museums and galleries there are people to tell you the story in an interesting way. There are museums of all kinds in London, from the big ones like the British Museum or those in South Kensington to small ones like the Horniman Museum at Forest Hill, whilst some of the boroughs have little local museums at their central libraries. There is not room in a book like this to tell you about all of them—the British Museum alone needs a book to itself—but we must mention a few of the more important ones.

First, of course, there is the British Museum in Bloomsbury. It was founded in the middle of the eighteenth century as a library for the books and manuscripts collected by Sir John Cotton and other gentlemen of that time, and for the natural history specimens and curios collected by Sir Hans Sloane. At first admission was by ticket only, but after the present building was erected the galleries were thrown open free. Besides the books and manuscripts in the reading-room for admission to which tickets are still necessary, there are many rooms of pictures and prints, collections illustrating Chinese and Eastern civilizations, and the great galleries showing the growth of civilization from the very earliest days of the Old Stone Age down to the end of the Saxon period in England. Perhaps the most interesting and beautiful things in the whole museum are the sculptures from the Parthenon at Athens and the collection of Greek vases. In the library there are many famous books and documents including a copy of Magna Carta.

The story of Western civilization is continued through the Middle Ages at the Victoria and Albert Museum at South Kensington, where there are all sorts of interesting things—costumes, pictures and sculpture, this last includ-

THE BRITISH MUSEUM

ing one of the loveliest things in the world, a little boy
as Cupid, carved by Michael Angelo himself. The
Science Museum with its models of machinery is perhaps
the most interesting to boys (although I have taken groups
of girls there and found it almost impossible to get them
away). The Natural History Museum, which among
other things tells us the story of life on the earth before
man began to write history, is another wonderful place.

Our own museum, devoted entirely to the history of
London, is the London Museum at Lancaster House,
St. James's. The house itself is one of London's historic
buildings and is so magnificent that Queen Victoria once
said that coming to it from Buckingham Palace was like
coming from a house to a palace. There is another
London museum at the Guildhall, and there are several
smaller general museums in different parts of London.

But enough of museums, for we must think of some of the picture galleries. I suppose that to most of you " pictures " means the cinema. That, too, was a London invention, for the first motion picture in the world was taken in Hyde Park in 1889. The inventor was Mr. Friese Green, a Londoner born in Bristol. The very first film shown to the public was at the Regent Street Polytechnic in 1896. But in this chapter I am thinking of paintings and drawings. Some of the world's greatest artists were either born in London or became Londoners by living there, and some of the world's greatest pictures were painted in London. No city in the world is richer in great paintings ; and none, not even Florence, Paris, or Vienna is more suited to the study of art or has better schools.

In the National Gallery there is some of the best work of the great artists of all countries, including that of Leonardo da Vinci, and of Michael Angelo. There is the work of the great British artists at the Tate Gallery, and at South Kensington ; there is the fine collection of naval pictures at the Royal Maritime Museum in Greenwich ; and there are many paintings of the very first class in the Wallace Collection, at Dulwich and at Ken Wood House. London, too, is a great musical and theatrical centre, with some of the finest choirs, orchestras and companies of actors in the whole world. A book could be written about the famous writers, dramatists and composers who have lived and worked there.

At the head of all this there is the University of London with its Colleges and its students from all parts of the world. Unlike the students at Oxford or Cambridge, most of those in London either live at home or in lodgings or hostels ; but a university is a place where every branch of learning may be studied and this can be done at London quite as well as at the older universities.

The first idea for a university in London came from Sir Thomas Gresham. He left his fortune to found a college in the city where the young merchants could learn

St. James's Palace

something more than just how to make money, but nothing came of the idea, although some lectures were started and are still carried on. So for centuries the only places of higher education in London were at the Temple and the other Inns of Court where barristers are trained ; but about a century ago two colleges, University College in Gower Street and King's College in the Strand, were started ; and a little later an examining body called the University of London was set up. From these small beginnings there has grown up one of the greatest universities in the world.

Before we finish this part of the chapter I should like you to read what John Milton, himself a Londoner, wrote at the beginning of the great Civil War in the middle of the seventeenth century :

" Behold now this vast city, [he says,] a city of refuge, the mansion house of liberty. The shop of war hath not more hammers and anvils working to fashion out plates and instruments of armed justice in defence of beleaguered truth than there be pens and heads there sitting by their studious lamps musing, searching, revolving new notions and ideas . . . others as fast reading, trying all things, asssenting to the voice of reason."

Do you think this is true of London to-day ?

In this chapter on health of body and mind we must not forget the parks. In a big place like London, where the country is so far away, parks and open spaces are very important. London has some very large ones, but unfortunately there are very few where they are most needed, in the crowded areas of the East End and the riverside boroughs. In rebuilding London it will be necessary to provide more open spaces in these crowded districts. Something had already been done during the nineteenth century when the Victoria Park was made in Bethnal Green, Battersea Park on Battersea Marsh and Southwark Park in Rotherhithe. At the same time a number of smaller spaces were saved from the builder, and larger spaces like Hampstead Heath, Blackheath, Clapham Common and Wimbledon Common were

I

IN REGENT'S PARK

secured.   Epping Forest, Hayes Common and some other
open spaces farther out were saved by the action of the
City Corporation in the middle of the century.

From its early days, too, the London County Council
was very active in securing parks for the public, buying
up the grounds of large houses within the county.   In
this way Brockwell Park, Ruskin Park, Peckham Rye
Park, Ken Wood and Avery Hill became public property.

The largest of all London's parks is the stretch of
parkland from Westminster to Kensington known as the
Royal Parks.   These form a continuous stretch of country
right in the heart of London and together they give a
country walk of over three miles with hardly a house to
be seen in the whole distance.   Here sheep graze as
though they were in the country, wild-fowl nest on the
lakes, and there are some lovely views through the trees ;
especially in Kensington Gardens, by the Serpentine in

Hyde Park and from the bridge over the lake in St. James's Park. These parks do not belong to the public in quite the same way as those managed by the L.C.C. They are the property of the Crown, for they were once the gardens of Royal palaces, but at various times they were opened to the public by our Sovereigns, as were also other Royal Parks at Greenwich, Regent's Park and Richmond Park. The Royal Parks are controlled by the Ministry of Works, a Government department responsible to Parliament.

Many changes have been made in the parks during recent years. At first they were kept merely as gardens where people were restricted to paths, even the grass being railed off. Then bandstands were built and concerts were given, flower-beds were laid out, and people were even allowed to sit on the grass. Later cricket and football were permitted and spaces were set apart for pitches ; then tennis became popular and tennis courts were laid out. After the First World War children's playgrounds were made, open-air swimming-pools were built, sunbathing enclosures set out and a great deal more was done to make the parks really useful as well as ornamental. When slum clearances were made, part of the site was set aside as a children's playground or as a rest garden, and in this way some sort of open space was saved in the more crowded districts.

Another interesting scheme was the " Green Belt." A hundred years ago an almost continuous belt of open country could have been saved round London at about four miles from Charing Cross ; at the beginning of this century it was still possible some ten miles out. In 1914 it could have been done fifteen miles from the centre ; to-day it would have to be very much farther out and even then it could not be continuous. But so important is this belt now considered that in 1938 the L.C.C. decided to spend a very large sum of money in helping the local authorities outside the county to buy up existing tracts of open country or farmlands and so prevent the builder getting hold of them.   By the end of 1938 a large, but very broken, ring had been formed.   More would have been done but for the war, and the Council proposes to carry on the scheme so as to get outside London an almost continuous belt of country that can never become town.

Another very great London treasure is to be found in the squares.   You have already read how these came to be built; now we will see how they were saved for the public only a few years ago.

During the early part of the nineteenth century when wealthy people lived in the houses, the squares were safe as open spaces, although they were terribly dull and neglected, for only the residents were allowed to use them. But towards the end of the century, when the wealthy people no longer lived there, the houses in the squares had become offices and no one used the railed-off plots in the centre.   Then, as land in the centre of London became more valuable, many fine old houses were pulled down and blocks of modern offices were erected.   The builders even began to cast envious eyes on the squares themselves and they would soon have been closed and built over.   But the L.C.C. stepped in and, after a lot of trouble, secured an Act of Parliament which saved the squares from the builder and so kept a good deal of open space where it was most needed, besides preserving for London one of its most beautiful features.   Many of the squares are terribly neglected still, and they need a lot of work put into them before they can really be called beautiful, but at least they are safe.

What of the future ?   Although London has a very large area of open space, especially in the extreme south-east and in the north-west, is now almost surrounded by a green belt and has wedges of country running in to within almost four miles of the centre, much remains to be done, especially in the riverside areas and in the East End.   Fortunately, however, we are now alive to the importance of parks and open spaces, so that in the plans for rebuilding after the war the provision of parks has not been forgotten.

In the *County of London Plan* it is proposed that the whole of London's open spaces, public and private, as well as all the land not yet built over shall be arranged to form a continuous system of parks. New parks would be made by clearing bombed sites or laying out undeveloped land and these would be linked up with those already existing by broad, tree-lined roads. The whole would be connected in the same way with the green belt. This would give London a most beautiful approach, for it would be possible to drive to within a mile or two of the centre from any direction through such parkways. The middle ring road, too, would be treated in the same way, linking up the parks by a wide, tree-lined, grass-bordered road forming a sort of lesser green belt round inner London. New open spaces will be made in the densely populated areas by rearranging the buildings, a fairly easy task as most of these districts have been pretty thoroughly cleared by bombing.

There remains the Thames, the largest open space in London, and, if treated properly, the most beautiful. The ideal would be to consider the whole course of the river within the county as a parkway and to border it on both banks with a wide embankment promenade lined with trees and bordered by grassy walks, with a fast motorway behind. Unfortunately this cannot be done because, in the lower reaches at least, the claims of commerce must be considered. The existing embankments show what could be done and in the chapter on the Thames we have discussed the plans that have been made for the future, and so we will not say anything more about them here.

London could be made one of the most beautiful cities in the world, without losing any of its importance as a commercial centre. The destruction caused by the war has given us the finest opportunity for doing this since the Great Fire, and we ought to make the most of it.

The opportunity was lost in 1666 because the planners spent too much time in talk. Whilst they talked, individual citizens rebuilt their premises on the same sites, and as the community as a whole was not interested in building a beautiful city, nothing was done. This time the chances of success are greater because the War lasted for so long that we had plenty of time for discussion and schemes both for immediate building and for long-term planning have been produced. It will take a long time to complete, but when it is finished London should be worthy of its history and traditions.

CHAPTER VIII

THE STREET OF INK

"WHEN you have seen one green field," said Dr. Johnson, "you have seen all green fields. Let's take a walk in Fleet Street." He thought Fleet Street was the very centre of the world, and in one way he was right ; it was impossible to walk from Temple Bar to Ludgate Circus without meeting some of the most important writers of that time and it is just as impossible to take the same walk to-day without passing some of the most important writers of our own time. Fleet Street is the street of ink, the home of the world's greatest newspapers. It is from Fleet Street that the ideas flow. There is just about a quarter of a mile of it, yet into that short distance is concentrated not only the great London papers, but also the London offices of others whose homes are in the provinces, in the United States of America and in every country of the world. Besides these there is a host of magazines and other publications too numerous to mention, all coming from this part of London. That quarter-mile is crowded with reporters, artists and writers, and in the streets opening out of it the clatter of the presses is never silent. Into it flows all the news, to be sorted out and fitted together to make the daily story of the world. By telegraph and telephone, by wireless, by the post and by messengers, the news flows in ; and by newspaper and booklet, by magazine and periodical, in print and in pictures, it goes out again, edited, arranged and displayed, to tell the whole world what to think and what to say.

Have you ever been into one of the great newspaper offices ? From most of them come both morning and evening papers, so that they are busy for the whole twenty-four hours, from the basement where the great presses live right up to the attics where the photographers, artists and illustrators work. What happens in these great buildings ?

As the news comes in—either as a simple statement that something has happened or as a report from a correspondent or a reporter—it is passed to the sub-editors' room where it is written up by one of the staff and sent on to the section to which it belongs—foreign news, home news, parliamentary reports, literary and dramatic criticism, or whatever it may be—and the editor of that section fits it in to the space he has at his disposal. Whilst this is being done the Art Editor decides what illustrations shall be used and orders the blocks, the Literary Editor makes up his columns, and the leader writers get their articles ready after reading the news material that is going into that issue. All this has to be done at great speed, as there is not much time to spare ; news must always be new. As each section is completed it is set up in type and a rough proof pulled which is sent up to the Editor-in-Chief who decides how much space each item shall have. When everything is settled the proofs go down to the linotype operators who set up the final form. This is then sent to the casting room where it is made into stereo blocks, half cylinders of metal which contain everything in one solid block ready to be fitted on to the great rotary presses. Meanwhile the machine-minders have been getting the presses ready, cleaning, oiling, and testing them, inking the rollers and putting the rolls of paper, each five miles long, on to their rollers at one end of the machine so that everything is ready when the signal to go comes down from the Editor. When the signal is given the current is switched on, for these machines are worked by electric power, the presses revolve, the long sheet of paper on the feed rolls begins to unwind and to disappear into the press, coming out at the other end as newspapers, printed, folded, counted and stacked ready to go up to the publishing office and from there to be sent by motor van, train, ship and 'plane to the newsagents in all parts of the world. The Press

FLEET STREET, SHOWING THE LAW COURTS ON THE LEFT AND
THE CHURCH OF ST. CLEMENT DANES ON THE RIGHT

137

to-day is one of the most powerful forces in the world. Not only do our newspapers tell us what is happening, but they tell us what they would like us to think about it all. The editors and the writers decide what we shall know about events and they form our opinions for us ; what Fleet Street says to-day the whole country will be thinking and talking about to-morrow.

Although Fleet Street has always been the home of printers it is only just over a century since the newspapers came there, the first being the *Morning Advertiser* in 1825. This was soon followed by the *Standard* and then came the *Evening Standard*. In 1846 the *Daily News* was started by Charles Dickens, and about ten years later came the *Telegraph*, one of the oldest news-

PRINTING A NEWSPAPER

papers in London, not so old as *The Times* but older than any other daily paper now issued in London. The *Daily Mail* was the first of the modern dailies, starting early in the present century, to be followed soon after by the *Daily Express* and the pictorial papers, the *Daily Mirror* and the *Daily Sketch*. These papers made a great impression, and very soon the older ones like the *Daily News* and the *Daily Chronicle* and even *The Times* and the *Telegraph* found it necessary to change their style, to have magazine pages and pictures, although it was a long time before they abandoned their old style of printing. The First World War had a great effect on the newspapers. Many of the older ones lost so many of their readers that they had to stop, and several of those that survived found it necessary to combine with others, so that to-day, in spite of all the newspapers that have been started during the present century, we have fewer dailies than our grandparents had. There are only three evening papers now where there used to be many more, and the number of morning papers is only about half what it once was.

Producing a newspaper is so much more expensive now than it was even a few years ago that only the very biggest companies, with millions of pounds of capital, can afford the risk; and even then the margin between success and failure is very narrow. It is only through their income from advertisements that papers can pay their way, and the advertisements depend on the circulation. If this drops by a few thousands then the advertisers take away their custom and the paper cannot afford to go on. So you can see why, before the War, the papers made so much of their advertising pages, especially of the big displays on the front page. The newspaper offices have now spread far beyond Fleet Street but all the larger and more important ones are somewhere in the neighbour-hood, and papers that really belong to other parts of the world generally have a London office with an editor there so that they may quickly print the opinions of the London Press.

The newspaper itself is quite a new thing, the first of the daily papers being the *Courant*, started in 1703; but the idea is a century older, dating from the times of James I when " Newsletters " began to be circulated. These were single sheets, sometimes written by hand, and they were produced at very irregular intervals. They contained just news items, often dealing with the move-ments of ships. Sometimes they had a letter from some merchant in a foreign town, but there were no leading articles or illustrations. Ben Jonson, in one of his plays,

The Staple of News, has an amusing account of the way in which the editors got their information. He pictures the editor and the printer setting up their office in a hollow tree and their messengers running in with bits of gossip they have gathered by listening at keyholes and peeping through cracks. Even Goldsmith in the eighteenth century had a very poor opinion of the newspapers of his day, for he says :

"You must not imagine that they who compile these papers have any actual knowledge of politics or the government of the State ; they only collect their materials from the oracle of some coffee-house, which oracle has himself gathered them from a beau, who had them from a great man's porter, who has had his information from the great man's gentleman, who invented the whole story for his own amusement."

The Great Civil War brought the political pamphlet, out of which grew the leading article ; and such publications as Steele's *Tatler* and Addison's *Spectator* gave rise to the magazine pages in our newspapers as well as to the magazines for which Fleet Street is also famous.

It is difficult to find a reason for this collecting of newspapers in Fleet Street. Perhaps it is because the printers were already there ; perhaps because the street connects London with Westminster, trade with politics ; perhaps because it lies so near the Temple ; for most of the early journalists, like many of them to-day, were barristers of the Inns of Court.

Many interesting stories could be told about the papers and magazines that have come from Fleet Street. Perhaps the best is that concerning Mr. Punch, the little humpback whose humorous comments everyone enjoys so much. He was born at No. 85 Fleet Street in the house where John Milton once taught in a school. Mark Lemon, Henry Mayhew and a few other writers met one evening to discuss the starting of a new paper which was to be a humorous review of the week's news. There was a lot of talk about the title when someone's fancy was caught by the sight of Mark Lemon slicing lemons into a bowl of hot punch he was getting ready. The name Punch jumped into his mind, was said with a funny reference to Mr. Lemon, and was immediately adopted. So we got our *Punch*. The little man himself is of course the hero of the Punch and Judy plays and really came from Italy, where he is Signor Punchinello. The paper was a failure at first, but was saved by W. M. Thackeray who wrote *Miss Tickletoby's History of England* for it and later, *Jeame's Diary*, and by Douglas Jerrold who wrote *Mrs. Caudle's Curtain Lectures*.

If the newspapers are newcomers to Fleet Street the printers were there almost from the beginning. They start in the fifteenth century with Wynkyn de Worde, who opened a printer's shop almost on the site of the *News Chronicle* office. From here he issued cheap reprints of popular books, books of riddles and fairy tales, school textbooks and the like, most of his schoolbooks having as their frontispiece the rather formidable picture of a schoolmaster armed with a big birch. Caxton at his press in Westminster printed expensive books for the rich, but de Worde started with the idea of making reading popular by printing books so cheaply that everyone could afford to buy them, and by making them so interesting that everyone would want to read them. Soon afterwards Pynson, another English printer, moved from St. Clement Danes in the Strand to a place in Fleet Street. Every reader should be grateful to him for it was he who gave up the old black letter type which is so difficult to read and introduced the roman type we use to-day for all our books, magazines and newspapers.

The booksellers did not come until after the Great Fire which burned them out of their old quarters around St. Paul's Cathedral and burned down most of Fleet Street too. When London was rebuilt many of the booksellers went to Paternoster Row, to be burned out again during the " blitz " of 1940–1 ; but many of them went to Fleet Street, especially round Temple Bar, where they were near the printers at the eastern end of the street, the writers who lived in the Temple and Lincoln's Inn, and their customers the courtiers and gentry of Westminster. There was no popular market for books then, and it was necessary for an author to have a patron who would guarantee the costs of printing and publishing or to find a number of subscribers who would promise to buy the book when it was printed. So the bookseller became the publisher, not only selling books in a shop but arranging all the details of their writing, printing and publication. Many of these early publishers were very famous men. There was Marsh, who published Stow's *Chronicle of London* in the reign of James I; Smethwick, who issued Shakespeare's *Hamlet* and *Romeo and Juliet*; Richard Marriott, who published the *Compleate Angler* written by his neighbour Izaak Walton, who owned a draper's shop at the corner of Fleet Street and Chancery Lane. In the Lane itself lived Jacob Tonson, who published Dryden's poems and whose chief claim to fame is that he was the first to issue Shakespeare's plays in a cheap and handy form. Near Temple Bar was the shop of Lintot, who published Gay's *Trivia*; and under the Middle Temple arch lived Mott, the publisher of *Gulliver's Travels*. Near by was Walker, the publisher who bought the manuscript of the *Paradise Lost* from John Milton for ten pounds.

Why do we mention all these names? Because to-day books and magazines are almost as necessary to us as clothes, and without the publisher there would be very few books. When an author has written a book he wants people to buy it and to read it, and so it has to be printed. Very few writers have either the time or the money for all the work that has to be done and paid for before a manuscript can become a printed book, and very few printers could afford the risk of printing, binding and advertising a book that might not sell enough copies to pay its cost. Besides, many books have to be illustrated, and someone has to decide as to the kind of paper that shall be used, the type for the printing, the binding, the advertising, the price, the distribution to the bookshops and a number of other matters about which the author usually knows very little and the printer less. All this is what the publisher does, and because he knows what the public wants to read, how to make books look attractive and how to advertise them, where to look for artists and printers, how to make the profits on one book pay for the losses on another, he is able to keep up a steady flow of books and to give us all plenty to read.

At first Fleet Street was merely a narrow lane joining Thames Street and the Strand, and it has no history until the thirteenth century when the bishops and abbots came to live there because it was near to the city and to the Court at Westminster. So along both sides of the way from the River Fleet to the Temple were the palaces of bishops and abbots, generally set back from the road with an inn in front where travellers could stay, for the medieval churchmen were supposed to find lodging for all travellers. On the river side of the road was the house of the Bishop of St. David's; then the nunnery of St. Bride with St. Bride's church and its holy well; next came the house of the Bishop of Salisbury, with a lane, marked now by John Carpenter Street, separating it from the Carmelite priory called Whitefriars which extended westwards to the Temple, from which it was separated only by a wall. The site of the priory is now covered by the offices of the *Daily Mail*, the *Evening News* and other newspapers, but during the seventeenth century it was the home of all sorts of bad characters; for when it was a priory there had been a right of sanctuary which prevented the officers of the city from arresting criminals who had taken refuge there, and this right was kept up after the monastery had disappeared. There is a good description of life in Alsatia, as the district was called, in *The Fortunes of Nigel* by Sir Walter Scott. Bits of the old Alsatia may still be seen by those who care to explore the district—Hanging Sword Alley is as narrow and tortuous as it was in the time of James I; and the

Harrow, a tavern that was once the resort of highwaymen, still exists. At various times underground cellars belonging to the priory have been found and there are probably still some yet to be discovered. Behind the north side of the street is a nest of courts and alleys, most of them the yards of inns before the Great Fire. These too were originally the property of churchmen, became ordinary taverns at the Reformation and were rebuilt after the Fire. On the ground covered by their yards houses were built, and some of the best examples of the kind of house that was built then can still be seen in these courts. The most famous of the courts are those connected with Dr. Johnson, who was so much at home in Fleet Street that his name cannot be kept out of anything written about it. His favourite seat could be seen in St. Clement Danes before it was destroyed by fire during the " blitz," and his most famous home was at No. 17 Gough Square where he lived whilst making his *Dictionary*. This is still kept as Dr. Johnson's house, filled with relics of the great man and open to the public. From Gough Square he moved to Staple Inn, Holborn, and then back again to Fleet Street, taking a house in Bolt Court, where he wrote *The Lives of the Poets* and where he died in 1779. The house is now the site of the L.C.C. School of Photo Engraving, but at No. 3, which survives, there lived a friend of Johnson's, a Dr. Lettsom,

OLIVER GOLDSMITH

whose country house at the top of Denmark Hill, Camberwell, was pulled down to make room for a block of L.C.C. dwellings only a few years ago. The doctor's prescriptions were always signed I. Lettsom, and somebody once wrote the following pun on the name :

> If any folk applies to I,
> I physics, bleeds and sweats 'em ;
> If after that they choose to die,
> Why, what cares I ?
> I. Letts 'em.

It was in Bolt Court that, " in a dark letter-box in a dark court," Charles Dickens dropped his first writing, a manuscript called *A Dinner at Poplar Walk*. Oliver Goldsmith lived in Wine Office Court where he wrote *The Vicar of Wakefield*, and here he met Dr. Johnson for the first time. I will tell you the story as Boswell tells it, giving Johnson's own words :

"I received one morning a message from poor Goldsmith that he was in great distress, and as it was not in his power to come to me, begging that I would come to him as soon as possible. I sent him a guinea and promised to come to him directly. I accordingly went as soon as I was dressed, and found that his landlady had arrested him for his rent, at which he was in a great passion. I perceived that he had already changed my guinea and had got a bottle of Madeira and a glass before him. I put the cork into the bottle, desired he would be calm and began to talk to him of the means by which he might be extricated. He then told me that he had a novel ready for the press, which he produced to me. I looked into it and saw its merit ; told the landlady I would soon return, and having gone to a bookseller, sold it for sixty pounds. I brought Goldsmith the money and he discharged his rent, not without rating his landlady in a high tone for having used him so ill."

There are many other associations between Fleet Street and the great writers, for Samuel Richardson, the first English novelist, was a printer living in Salisbury Square, Lovelace the poet lived in Shoe Lane, and Dryden in Fetter Lane.

The taverns of Fleet Street are also famous, for in them the writers met. The most interesting was that called "The Devil," just by St. Dunstan's Church. Originally

K

it was " The Devil and St. Dunstan," with a sign representing the Saint gripping the Devil by the nose with red-hot tongs.   Perhaps our phrase about going to the

DR. SAMUEL JOHNSON

Devil may have something to do with this inn, for it was a very popular place with the lawyers, who used to go there in the afternoon, first pinning to their doors the notice " Gone to The Devil " so that their clients might know where to find them.   It was at " The Devil " that Ben Jonson's famous club, the Apollo, used to meet.   The bust of Apollo that stood over the door of the meeting-room and the notice board with the verse :

Welcome all who lead or follow
To the oracle of Apollo ;
Here he speaks out of his pottle,
Or the tripos, his tower bottle.
All his answers are divine,
Truth itself doth flow in wine—

are still kept at Child's Bank which stands on the site of the tavern.

The " Olde Cheshire Cheese " is the tavern most associated with Dr. Johnson, although there is no mention by Boswell or by any other contemporary writer that he was ever there.   But tradition says that he was, and on the strength of this they show his favourite seat, and, during the winter, serve a pudding said to be made according to his recipe.   Because of this most writers of the nineteenth century have dined there, and of course the Americans, hosts of them, in spite of the fact that

Johnson himself hated Americans almost more than he hated Scotsmen.

Temple Bar is the end of Fleet Street and is the western boundary of the city. Originally there were posts and chains set up here to mark the city boundary, but these were soon followed by a gatehouse with strong wooden gates. After the Great Fire had destroyed the old gatehouse, a new one was built by Sir Christopher Wren; it had a wider gateway than the old one but was still an obstruction to traffic. Wren's gate remained until 1878, when it was taken down and given away by the Corporation. It was erected by Sir Henry Meux as the gate to his estate at Theobalds, near Waltham Cross. It is still there. As the boundary of the city, Temple Bar was one of the places where the heads or parts of the bodies of those executed for treason were set up, and here too the Sovereign has to ask permission to enter the city even if he is going to dine with the Lord Mayor. For the City of London is a republic whose president is the Lord Mayor, and the King may not enter without permission. When there were gates, these were closed with the Sovereign's procession outside and the Lord Mayor and his officers inside. Then the Royal Herald knocked and asked permission for his master to enter. This was granted, the gates opened and the keys offered to His Majesty who touched them and returned them to the Lord Mayor. The two monarchs, for the Lord Mayor is second only to the Sovereign when within the city, then proceeded side by side along Fleet Street, up Ludgate Hill and so to their destination. Although there is no longer a gate to shut, the ceremony is still kept up where the gate used to be, to remind everyone that London is a place apart from the rest of the Kingdom. The significance of the ceremony has long been lost in pageantry, but it is still there.

Of all the pageants staged at Temple Bar perhaps the most brilliant was that for the coronation of Queen Elizabeth. There was no ceremony of admission, for the

Queen was going out to Westminster escorted by the Lord Mayor, but the procession was halted so that she might take official farewell of the city. Outside stood the Queen's guard, but on the city side were the train-bands who had escorted her from the Tower, the Lord Mayor with the sheriffs and other officers, and of course crowds of people; whilst the liverymen of the guilds, all in new gowns and hoods, lined the road and their ladies filled the windows above. Figures of Gog, Magog and Corineus, the city giants, were posted on guard at the gate whilst the boys of the city churches, robed in their surplices, sang anthems from the roof and speeches were made in Latin, to which the Queen replied in the same language. The rest of the day was spent by the people in singing and dancing; bonfires were lighted at the gate and right along Fleet Street, and the fountains were made to spout wine instead of the usual water.

On the eastern side of the Bar, just over the gate to the Middle Temple, is one of the most interesting bits of Tudor London, a timber-fronted house known as Prince Henry's Room. Tradition says that Cardinal Wolsey ordered it to be built; but later on the long room over the gate was used as the council chamber of the Duchy of Cornwall, as the Prince of Wales was always the Duke of Cornwall, it would have been associated with Henry, Prince of Wales, son of James I and friend of Sir Walter Raleigh. During the eighteenth century the front was covered up with lath and plaster and sash windows were put in; and in the early part of the nineteenth century it was used as the home of Mrs. Salmon's Waxworks, the predecessor of Madam Tussaud's. During the widening of the street a few years ago the front of the building had to be taken down and then the original Tudor front was discovered. It was decided to restore the room as nearly as possible to its original condition. It was possible to do this as the original ceiling and much of the old panelling of the walls was still in position.

Whilst we are here we ought to go through the gateway

FOUNTAIN COURT, THE TEMPLE

into the Temple, the home of the lawyers and one of the
most beautiful spots in London. No other city in the
world has anything like it. Here the roar of London is
stilled although it is only a few yards away ; here is
the lovely Fountain Court with its trees and fountain,
the quaint Pump Court and the gardens bordering the
Embankment. It was in these gardens that the quarrel
broke out that started the Wars of the Roses, and in
them many famous men have walked. Between Fountain
Court and the gardens was the fine Elizabethan Hall of
the Middle Temple with a lovely roof and a table that

is said to have come from Drake's cabin in *The Golden Hind*. The Temple Church is the oldest part of all the buildings. It was built by the Knights Templars when they came here in 1185 and is a round church after the pattern of the Holy Sepulchre. On its floor there are the tombs of some of the men who forced King John to agree to the Magna Carta.

Fleet Street takes its name from the Fleet River. To-day this river runs underground, except for its sources in the Hampstead and Highgate Ponds on Hampstead Heath, but it used to be a clear, bright stream, tidal right up to Holborn. However, it soon began to get dirty when London was built and its condition became worse as the centuries passed until Pope was able to describe it as :

> Fleet Ditch with disembouging stream
> Rolls its large tribute of dead dogs to Thames,
> The king of dykes ! than whom no sluice of mud
> With deeper sable blots the silver flood.

Swift has an even more vivid picture of the stream swollen with rain, pouring down the refuse from Smithfield. Dead dogs and cats, offal from the butchers' stalls, vegetable and other rubbish all—

> Seem to tell
> What street they came from
> By their sight and smell.

Every attempt to cleanse it failed, and so they put it into a drain and made of it a stormwater sewer.

On its banks stood one of the most famous of all prisons, the Fleet, where you could be a prisoner and yet, if you had money, live as far away as the West Indies and carry on your ordinary business ; where you could get married at a moment's notice and get unmarried again just as quickly. In Stuart times it was used as a State prison for those who were not important enough to be sent to the Tower, but later it became a debtor's prison where it cost fifty pounds to get in and even more in fees to get out again. The prisoners were of two classes, those on the Common Side who could not afford to pay the boarding fees and got their living by begging, and those on the Master's Side who paid heavily for the privilege of a private room. For these, life in the prison was a fairly comfortable affair and, by paying extra fees, it was possible for the prisoner to get a licence to live " in the liberties," that is, in lodgings outside the prison. Because of this the Fleet was much sought after by shady financiers, who could get themselves arrested for a very small debt, be committed to prison, pay the fees for " liberty " and so avoid arrest for much larger sums. One story tells of a wine merchant who had himself arrested for a very small debt owed to one of his clerks. He refused to pay, was sent to prison and obtained licence to live " in the liberties." This enabled him to carry on his business and even to make voyages to France to buy wines. He paid cash for his purchases until his credit was established, and then ran up heavy bills which he failed to pay. His creditors began proceedings against him only to discover that he was already a prisoner, who could not be sued again.

Outside the prison itself was a district called "the rules," extending from the river back to Holborn and from St. Paul's to St. Bride's. In this area lived those prisoners who were " in the liberty " and also many others who were able to claim the freedom from arrest that inmates of the Fleet possessed. Here too lived those disreputable parsons who would perform marriage ceremonies for a small fee, even providing the bride or the bridegroom, and who were quite willing, for another small fee, to tear up the certificate and forget the whole business. The whole area is still one of the most dreary in all London and seems to retain something of the characters of the shady individuals who used to live there in the days of the prison.

CHAPTER IX

OLD FATHER THAMES

IN the earlier chapters of this book you read how
London began and why it grew up just where it is.
It was the Thames that made London, and it is to the
Thames that she owes her present importance. London
to-day is the commercial capital of the world. It is
the Thames that has made her so, and the right way to
approach the city and so to see her commerce is to come
up the river from the sea. Passing the stream of shipping in the lower reaches, and steaming up between
banks lined with wharves and warehouses, dodging
barges and lighters, and finally passing under Tower
Bridge into the Upper Pool, we see London as she really
is : the daughter of Old Father Thames. The Londoners
of the time of James I knew this very well, for on one
occasion when they had refused to lend money to the
King, James threatened that he would take himself and
his Court away from London and so ruin their city.
The citizens listened to the King with respect, but when
he had finished the Lord Mayor replied : " Your Majesty
hath the power to do what you please, and your City of
London will obey accordingly ; but when your Majesty
shall remove your Court she humbly desires that you
would be pleased to leave the Thames behind you."
The greatness of London depended on the Thames and
not on the presence of the King and his Court.

The Thames in London is now a dirty brown stream
flowing swiftly between banks lined with wharves and
warehouses, crossed by numerous bridges and little used
except for commerce ; but in former days it was clear
and bright, flowing between green banks past riverside
villages, and famous for its fish which included salmon
and sturgeon. In the Middle Ages old London Bridge
with its narrow arches formed a dam that held up the

water and made a wide lake above the bridge. This lake was bordered by the palaces of kings, nobles, and bishops, and was crowded with boats and barges; for in those days the river was the great highway, and everyone who had to travel from Westminster to London went by water. So on the river all the sights were to be seen. There was the King in his barge attended by guards and courtiers; there were the barges of the great nobles, the galleys of the City Companies, and the rowboats of the humbler citizens, for people then went on the river as we go for a walk in the park. In the evenings, too, there were sports. A shield was fastened to a pole and set up in the river, and an apprentice, armed with shield and lance and standing on a narrow platform raised on stilts above a rowboat, would be carried down by the force of the tide towards the pole. His task was to strike the shield, which was hung from one end of a bar pivoted on the post, in such a way that when the shield was struck the bar swung round, and unless the boy were very nimble he was knocked into the water by a sandbag on the other end of the bar. The same thing happened if he missed, for then the force of his blow carried him overboard. We can imagine the jeers of his friends as he was fished up out of the water and carried dripping ashore. Another game was for two young men armed with shield and lance to be carried against each other by boats something like knights in a tournament, each trying to knock the other into the water.

In winter, should there be a severe frost, the scene was changed; for the river above bridge, not being troubled by the tide, soon froze over, and then Ice Fairs were held. This happened only once or twice in each century, so that people never got tired of the novelty and on each occasion they tried to outdo the last. One of the greatest of these fairs took place in 1683. The frost began early in December and lasted until the end of February. The river soon froze over, and when the ice was strong enough a regular street of shops was set up from Westminster down to London Bridge.   There were booths where oxen were roasted ; carts and carriages passed to and fro as in a street ; there was a printing press where people had their names and verses of poetry printed.   There was skating and sliding, bull baiting, coach racing and even a theatre where plays were performed.   The last of these Ice Fairs took place in the early days of Queen Victoria's reign, for soon afterwards the new bridge was built. Although there have been one or two great frosts since then, the river has never frozen over ; for the rise and fall of the tide quickly breaks up and carries away any ice that may form.

When the river was the most important highway in London there were large numbers of watermen who carried passengers and of lightermen who carried goods up and down the river or from the ships anchored in the river to the wharves and warehouses on the banks.   There are still a large number of lightermen but very few watermen as there is hardly any passenger traffic now and the members of the two trades have combined into one Guild. But the watermen used to have their own guild and they had their own poet too, John Taylor who lived in the reign of James I.   As he had a station opposite the Bankside, he must often have carried Shakespeare and Ben Jonson across the river to the theatres in Southwark.   Taylor was a great traveller.   On one occasion he rowed from London to York and on another from London to Hereford, but as there were no canals in those days he must have carried his boat across from one river to another, unless he went by sea, as he says he did in a journey to Salisbury.   Coaches were just coming into use in Taylor's time, and he was very angry about the way they took passengers away from the watermen.

In 1715 Thomas Doggett, the actor, instituted the annual race for Doggett's Coat and Badge.   The race was held in honour of the House of Hanover and to commemorate the accession of George I.   It is still rowed each year, on the first of August, and is between the best six of the watermen who have completed their apprenticeship and been admitted to the guild during the past year. The course was formerly from the Old Swan Stairs at London Bridge to the Old Swan Stairs at Chelsea, but as both sets of stairs have disappeared it is now rowed from the Old Swan Pier to the Cadogan Pier just past Chelsea Bridge. The prize is a scarlet coat with a silver armplate bearing the white horse of Hanover. Each competitor also gets a money prize.

From the middle of the fifteenth century down to the middle of the nineteenth the Thames was famous for its pageants : some gay, others sad. One of the first to be held was when Eleanor Cobham, Duchess of Gloucester, was condemned to do public penance for witchcraft. She had to go from Westminster to St. Paul's Cathedral wearing only a white linen nightdress and carrying a lighted candle. As the Thames was the most public place in London she was taken by water from Westminster to the Temple on the first day, which was the 13th of November, to Old Swan Stairs on the 15th, and to Queenhithe on the 17th, finishing the journey each day on foot.

A few years later John Norman, the new Lord Mayor, decided that his Show should go by water, and the river was always part of the route of the Lord Mayor's Show until 1855, when the Lord Mayor's barge, *Maria Wood*, was used for the last time. There is a model of this barge in the Guildhall Museum. All that time the City companies kept their barges which were used in the Show, and on other occasions too, and the processions were very grand affairs, for, besides the barges of the companies with their members in their robes, there were the train-bands, barges carrying pageants and all the things that go to the making of the Lord Mayor's Show.

Boats that had to go below bridge often had an exciting time ; for, if the tide were out, there was a considerable difference in the level of the water and the rapids were dangerous. Most people went ashore above bridge and walked round, leaving their boatmen to shoot the bridge ; but sometimes a gentleman would decide to run the risk and there was a spill. It must have been quite exciting to the people on the bridge when this happened, and the great man and his attendants had to be pulled out of the river with boathooks and hauled up on to the bridge by the cranes that were used for landing goods.

With several royal palaces on the banks of the river there was always a great coming and going of the Court, especially in Tudor times ; on most occasions the King was escorted by the Lord Mayor and the aldermen and was entertained with pageants and music. Anne Boleyn, dressed in white, with a barge full of maids of honour and escorted by the King and the whole Court went up from Greenwich for her coronation at Westminster ; and, as she was the granddaughter of one Lord Mayor and niece of another, we may be sure the citizens vied with each other in giving her a welcome. Only a short while afterwards she made the same journey again, this time as a prisoner going for trial. After she was condemned she was taken to the Tower for execution by the same way, sitting opposite to the executioner, who faced her with the sharp edge of his axe turned towards her. Sir Thomas More must often have made that journey from his house at Chelsea to the Law Courts at Westminster or to see the King at Whitehall or Greenwich. He, too, made his last journey that way, unjustly condemned for treason, the greatest Londoner and one of the noblest Englishmen of all time.

Queen Elizabeth was always on the river ; so were James I and Charles I. We have an account of the journey of the latter with his Queen soon after their accession :

The King and Queen in the Royal barge with many other barges of honour and thousands of boats passed through London Bridge to Whitehall ; infinite numbers besides these in wherries, standing in ships, lighters, western barges and on the shore. The barge windows

THE THAMES AT GREENWICH

being open in spite of the rain and all the people shouting she put out her head and shaked it unto them.

Besides these processions there were masks and pageants. Handel's *Water Music* was written for one of these. The last pageant to take place on the Thames was that arranged to celebrate the peace in 1919. One of the most magnificent of the pageants was that arranged by the lawyers of the Temple during the reign of James I. It is described in these words by one of the students who saw it :

"The maskers, with their whole train in good order and all triumphant manner, took barge at Winchester Stairs and rowed to Whitehall against the stream : the chief maskers went in the King's barge royally adorned and plentifully furnished with such a large number of wax lights that they alone made a glorious show ; other gentlemen went in the prince's barge and were led by two admirals. Besides all these there were four lusty war-like galleys ; each barge and galley being replenished with store of torchlights made so rare and brave a show upon the water as the like was never seen upon the Thames."

We do not do anything like that now. One reason is that when old London Bridge was destroyed the river could flow freely and the former wide stretch of still water gave place to the present tidal stream with its swift current, its wide stretches of mud, and its shallow river at low water. So the river within London is hardly used at all for pleasure, although during the summer months there are steamers going up from Westminster to Hampton Court and a few launches take people down to the Tower Bridge. During the nineteenth century there were steamboats plying between Greenwich and London Bridge and a service of " Penny Steamers " ran from Chelsea down to London Bridge and Greenwich, but as the river became more and more crowded with shipping the steamers became less popular and they were withdrawn. The same fate overtook the attempt made by the L.C.C. at the beginning of this century. Special fast boats were built, piers were repaired and a service started ; but it soon failed and the

SIR THOMAS MORE
(*After a painting by Holbein*)

steamers were sold. English weather is so uncertain in the summer and so wet in the winter, and river traffic is so slow that all the pleasure has gone from travel on the water although there are few better ways of seeing London.

The decline in the use of the Thames for pleasure was beginning in the reign of James I, when Taylor, the waterman poet, wrote against tobacco and coaches; and it went on rapidly after the Restoration, when the merchants began to live in the country, the nobles had deserted their palaces along the Strand for new houses in fashionable St. James's and Soho Squares, and the pastures of Lambeth were filling up with warehouses.

You would think me [wrote the French traveller, D'Avenant, in the reign of Charles II,] a malicious traveller if I should still gaze on your mis-shapen streets and forget the beauty of your river; therefore I will pass the importunate noise of your watermen and step into one of your peascod boats whose tilts are not so sumptuous as gondolas. The trade of your river belongs to yourselves; but give me leave to share in the pleasure of it, which will hardly be in the prospect or in the freedom of the air, unless the prospect consist in here a palace, there a woodyard; here a garden, next a brewhouse; here a nobleman, next a dyer. If freedom of air be inferred where every man is at liberty to smoke out a magistrate, then the air of your Thames is free indeed.

The prospect is very little better to-day, in spite of the many improvements that were made during the nineteenth century, for the Surrey side is still crowded with dingy wharves, dilapidated warehouses and smoky chimneys. Even in the city the warehouses are allowed to crowd right down to the water's edge and to spoil the fine views of the city that could otherwise be obtained.

Yet the Thames in London, with its wide sweeping curves, the constantly changing view as one goes up or downstream, the beauty of the skyline broken by distant hills, the spires of churches or the roofline of buildings, gives one of the finest views in the world. And London could be made a worthy setting for this lovely river.

Something has already been done in the building of the three Embankments. When old London Bridge was pulled down, the wider arches of the new bridge allowed the water to run down freely, and the wide lake that used to exist gave place to a narrow stream bordered with stretches of bad-smelling mud, especially at low tide. The smells from this mud were so bad that people could no longer live near the river, and the rooms on the river side of the Houses of Parliament could not be used during the summer months. Something had to be done, and so, after years of talk, it was decided to set up a body of commissioners who were to do something to improve matters. The Metropolitan Board of Works was the result and one of its first tasks was the building of the three Embankments, the Victoria, from Blackfriars to Westminster Bridges, the Albert, from Westminster to Lambeth opposite to the Houses of Parliament, and the Chelsea, from Chelsea Bridge to Battersea Bridge. This last, with the old houses of Cheyne Row at the back and Battersea Park opposite, shows how beautiful the Thames could be made to look. But the Park only goes half-way, and beyond the Albert Bridge there is an ugly stretch of factories and wharves that completely spoils the view. The County Hall too shows something of what King's Reach would look like if the Lambeth bank were properly planned.

Many schemes have been put forward for improving

the banks of the river but they have all failed because of the great value of the sites on the banks for wharves and warehouses. Below the Tower Bridge it may be necessary for some of these to be right down on the water's edge so that the larger ships can discharge without the delay consequent on passing through the locks into a dock basin ; but above that point there would seem to be no real reason for warehouses at all. Goods have to be sent up by lighters and then distributed from the warehouses by road or rail; they could equally well be distributed direct from the down-river wharves, thus saving the extra cost of transhipment into lighters and the slow journey up river. But if there must be warehouses above the bridge they could easily be set back from the river, with subways for the barges to go under the embankment ; and the buildings themselves could be made to look beautiful instead of ugly and dirty, and be placed where they would improve rather than spoil the view. So many of the riverside buildings have been destroyed or badly damaged that the whole must be rebuilt after the war. It should therefore be a fairly easy matter to replan the whole of both banks of the river from Woolwich to Hammersmith and to redesign the warehouses so that they are at least not ugly.

This is what the *County of London Plan* proposes to do. Wharves and factories would be regrouped, mainly in the marshes at Greenwich, along the Isle of Dogs, and in Wandsworth ; the riverside space thus gained being used for open spaces from which fine views of the river could be seen, or for well-designed groups of office or residential buildings. Such warehouses as were allowed would be set back in line with the other buildings and made to conform to the general design. It suggests a complete replanning of the Surrey side from Vauxhall Bridge to London Bridge, where most of the area has been so badly damaged by bombs that it will have to be rebuilt in any case. There would be new bridges at the Temple and Charing Cross, the railways would cross the

L

river by tunnels and there would be a wide embankment right along the river backed by fine public buildings or blocks of offices, with the whole of the semicircle right back to its centre at the Elephant and Castle replanned and rebuilt. Along the river there would be tree-lined embankments with a promenade and a road behind. The rest of the river-bank would have an embankment road with blocks of well-designed offices or flats, broken, at those points from which the best views can be obtained, by parks and gardens.

This scheme would take several years to complete but much of it could be started at once, and if the architects would give us designs for the buildings that were worthy of the setting we should see London's river in all its beauty.

The river below London Bridge has always been the port of London, and, although the Port of London Authority now controls the whole of the river from Teddington to the Nore, the real port is still the part below the bridge. In Roman and medieval times the port was only that part between London Bridge and the Tower, the Pool of London ; and it was controlled by the city ; the Lord Mayor is still " Admiral of the Thames." Gradually, as ships became larger and trade increased, the port was extended down the river until it reached to Wapping, where Execution Dock marked its end. Here pirates were executed by drowning. They were chained to a post in the river is such a way that the tide would cover them, and left there for three tides. There were then no docks, the ships being anchored in the river, and all goods on which duties had to be paid were taken off and landed at certain quays. In 1559 the Custom House was founded at Billingsgate so that the whole business of collecting duties might be made easy, and all the invoices and bills of lading had to be sent there. This was all right when ships were small and all of them lay in the Pool, but as the ships got bigger and trade grew they had to lie farther and farther down the

THE HEAD OFFICE OF THE PORT OF LONDON AUTHORITY

river, the Indiamen right down at Blackwall. Their cargoes had then to be discharged into lighters which often took weeks to get up the river to the quays by the Pool and much of the cargo disappeared on the way. To remedy this, plans were made for building docks where the ships could enter and discharge direct to the warehouses. These docks were surrounded by high walls to keep out thieves, and often there was a screen of tall trees to break the wind which was a danger to the highmasted sailing ships tied up in the basins. It was not until the early years of the nineteenth century that anything was done. Then the West India Dock was built, followed soon after by the East India Dock for the general trade with the Far East, the Millwall Dock for the ships of the East India Company, the London and St. Catherine's Docks near the Tower for smaller ships, and the Surrey Docks at Rotherhithe, which were mostly used by the corn and timber ships from the Baltic and America. During the present century these docks have all been deepened and enlarged and great new ones built—the Royal Docks and the Tilbury Docks—so that the very largest ships can now use the port of London.

Until 1909 all the wharves and docks were privately owned and there was much competition and confusion. To end this, the Port of London Authority was set up and took control of all the docks and of the river, leaving the wharves still in the hands of private owners. The Authority is a public body whose business is not to make profits but to make a port, and its members are chosen not by public election but by the various bodies using the Port. Since its creation it has built beautiful new offices on Tower Hill, has deepened the river, increased the accommodation in the docks and their warehouses, and introduced all sorts of schemes for helping merchants. It will store, sort, grade and pack your goods, arrange for their sale by auction or otherwise, and generally do everything that an agent would do. This is a very great convenience, especially for the smaller merchants who could not afford to keep their own warehouses, and it has attracted a lot of trade to London, making it the greatest port in the world.

Although the business of collecting duties, not only for London but for the whole country, is still managed by the Custom House, goods no longer have to be landed on the wharf there and wait until the duty is assessed, for the system of bonded warehouses saves all that. These are warehouses under the control of the Customs' officer and goods stored in them pay duty only if they are brought out into this country; if they are taken out to be shipped abroad no duty is payable. This system makes our ports " free " and is of great benefit to London which is as much a European as it is a British port. The Thames is really the deep-water end of the great Rhine-Danube and Baltic routes; big ships can use it with much greater safety than they can use the Continental ports, and so European merchants have their goods sent to London and then transhipped to their destination by small coasters or even barges, some of which, motor barges of as much as two thousand tons, go right into the heart of Europe. All this is made possible by the situation of London and by the work of the P.L.A.

Some very good stories are told of the working of the Custom House in the past and one of them is very amusing. About a hundred years ago the first cargo of ice was brought to London from Norway, and as no one knew what the duty would be, or indeed if there were any duty to pay, the ice was stacked up on the quay at the Custom House whilst the Customs' officials, the Treasury and the Board of Trade made up their minds. The ice was landed in March and the whole summer passed in correspondence between the three departments, the officials trying to decide whether ice was a natural product or a foreign manufactured good. Finally they decided to class it with dry goods but by this time the ice had settled the matter for itself by melting and running away into the river.

London has many rivers besides the Thames.   At one time most of these were important little streams taking barges some distance inland or providing water for such trades as the leather industry of Bermondsey, but except for three they are now all underground.   You have already read about the Fleet.   The Walbrook flows right across the city from Moorgate to the Thames at Cannon Street Station, and was once an important part of the port, barges going up to as far as the site of the Mansion House where the remains of a Roman wharf were discovered.   All the other little rivers were in the country round the city and were gradually covered in as London grew, until only the Ravensbourne, the Lea and the Wandle are left.

The Wandle rises in the meadows about Cheam and Carshalton, and, after flowing through Mitcham, it enters the Thames at Wandsworth where its tidal mouth is still used by barges going to the paper mills, paint works and other factories on its banks.   During the French wars of the eighteenth century it was a busy stream, for large numbers of cannon were being cast at Croydon and carried down the Wandle in barges to be shipped from Deptford where there was the Royal Dockyard.

The Ravensbourne is still an important little river, rising on Keston Common and flowing down through Lewisham to Deptford, where it enters the Thames by Deptford Creek which is tidal and is much used by small colliers and coasters, as well as by the river steamers that used to go down to Margate, and by the ships of the General Steam Navigation Company that were in the Mediterranean fruit trade.

The Lea forms the eastern boundary of the county of London.   It rises in the Chiltern Hills near Luton, flows east past Hertford and then turns south to form the boundary, first between Essex and Middlesex, and then between Essex and London, entering the Thames by Barking Creek.   Its lower course is crowded with chemical, engineering and other factories, with the great

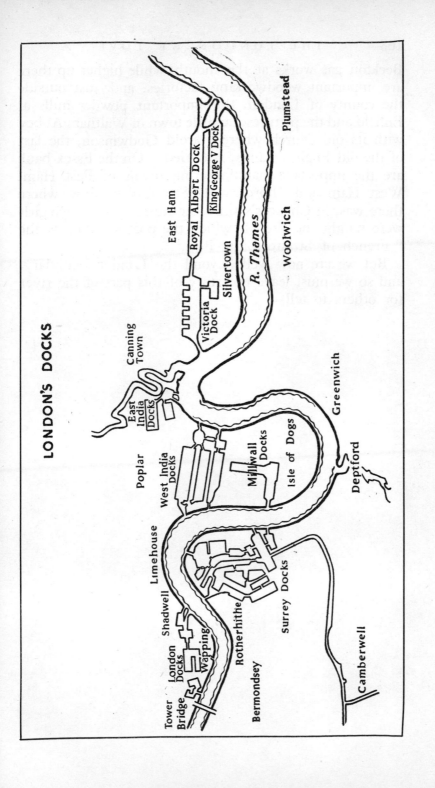

LONDON'S DOCKS

Beckton gas works at the mouth, while higher up there are important woodworking factories, and, just outside the county of London, the important powder mills at Enfield and the picturesque little town of Waltham Abbey with its old church where Harold Godwinson, the last of the old English Kings, is buried. On the Essex bank are the important manufacturing towns of East Ham, West Ham and Ilford, with Stratford-by-Bow where there was, in Chaucer's time, the nunnery in which girls were taught the French which the poet satirizes as the " French of Stratford-atte-Bow."

But we are now well beyond the London boundary, and so we must leave the story of this part of the river for others to tell.

CHAPTER X

THE GOLDEN GRASSHOPPER

LONDON is to-day the greatest commercial and financial city in the world. How did she get to this position, and why has she been able to hold it for so long in the face of great opposition from other cities? Partly it is because Londoners are a mixture of peoples from all parts of the world and have known how to make the most of the advantages for trade that their city gives them, but chiefly it is because of its situation that London is so important.

The city, which is the heart of London and the centre of its trade, stands at the lowest point at which the Thames can be crossed by bridges and at the highest point to which ocean-going ships can get up the river. It therefore stands on a busy crossing and this makes it an important place. More important still, however, is the position of the Thames itself. The river almost divides England into two, and its mouth is opposite the entrances to the two great trade routes across Europe, the Rhine-Rhone and the Rhine-Danube valleys. By these two routes all the trade across Europe must go. They meet on the lower Rhine and all trade to Britain from them must go through London. It was this that made London important in the first place.

The city began its life as a commercial centre. The remains of Roman London show that it traded even then with the south of France and with the Rhineland, for amongst the earliest relics is a great deal of Samian pottery which we know was made in the neighbourhood of Marseilles. There is also a great deal of Cologne ware amongst the bits of broken crockery that we dig up from the Roman level. We know too that, when Boudicca rebelled, London was full of traders who must have come from the Continent. So even in those early days

London was an important European port, and as the west of Europe became more civilized and its trade grew, so the importance of London would grow with it, until by the fifteenth century it had become one of the most important ports in the world.

For many centuries London had serious rivals, especially Antwerp ; but it had many advantages which its rivals lacked. The greatest of these were its freedom from outside interference and its freedom from war. From the time of William the Conqueror no king ever seriously interfered with London's freedom to govern itself, although many tried to do so. Sooner or later, however, each attempt failed, and after each one the city reappeared, not only with all its ancient rights but even with new ones added. From the time of the Danish invasions London was free from attack, chiefly because her citizens were always ready to defend themselves and were always able to do so. For from the time when the men of London marched out to defend their city against the Jutes at Grayford in A.D. 457 down to the time when they manned the A.A. guns against German aircraft and flew the Spitfires in the Battle of Britain, Londoners have always been ready to fight, not only for their own freedom but for that of others. Sometimes they have been beaten but never have they been defeated. They have always kept up the fight until the enemy gave in. London's rivals, the great towns of the Rhine mouths, have suffered again and again from the attacks of the invader ; London has always escaped without crippling damage ; indeed, until the two world wars of our own time, without damage at all. Her only invaders have been peaceful merchants and these were welcomed because they brought trade with them and themselves soon became Londoners.

It was the " new discoveries " of the fifteenth century that really made London great, because they brought world trade to Europe and there is no port so well placed for world trade in the whole of the continent.

Until the discovery of the sea route to India and the opening up of America all trade from outside Europe had gone through the Mediterranean Sea, although even in the Middle Ages the Low Countries and the Rhineland were the most important manufacturing districts in Europe and so took most of its trade. But when the spices of the East and the gold of America began to come from over the ocean they had to come direct to the Rhine, and it was soon found that the ports at the mouths of this river were not so well placed as was London. The prevailing winds in this part of the world come from the west and the Rhine flows out through a sandy delta right against them. So the ports at the mouth of the Rhine afforded, at that time, little shelter to the oceangoing ships against these westerly winds. But the Thames estuary was sheltered and gave safe anchorage for the largest ships, whilst goods could be transhipped across to Europe by coasters that could get right up the rivers into the heart of the industrial areas. So, in spite of the great efforts made by the Dutch, the big ocean ships preferred the safe waters of the Thames ; especially as they were not likely to be interfered with by hostile armies, nor, after the founding of the Royal Navy, by pirates in the Channel. Even during the Middle Ages London had maintained a navy of her own and she continued to do so after the building of the Royal Navy ; for the ships of the East India Company were well armed, and the Company also had regular warships to protect its merchantmen against attack. From the beginnings of ocean trade right down to the present day London has carried on a great trade, and she will continue to do so for so long as Western Europe is prosperous. This great commercial power has been used by London for the good of the whole world and we Londoners may well be proud, not only of the great wealth and the great trade of our city, but of the unselfish way in which that wealth has been used.

Another reason for the growth of trade in London is

the welcome she has always given to foreign merchants. Craftsmen from abroad were not always welcomed; they were often treated rather badly by the London craftsmen; but from the very earliest times there have always been a good many foreign merchants in the city and many of her most important citizens have come from abroad. There were Baltic merchants from Hamburg and Lubeck; men of Cologne and merchants from Flanders and Normandy in London before the Norman Conquest; and these were soon followed by Frenchmen from Paris and the south, Spaniards, Italians and merchants from even as far away as Constantinople. Most of them soon became Londoners and learned to look upon the city as their native land.

The most important English export in the Middle Ages was wool, and the trade was in the hands of the Florentines and the Lombards who were settled in the neighbourhood of Lombard Street, making that part of London the centre of the banking industry. Besides these there were the Hansards, a league of German merchants who did a large trade in timber, hemp, tar and other things from the Baltic countries. It was they who imported German iron and armour, then the best in Europe; and their hall, the Steelyard, was in Ironmonger Lane. Here they lived together in a walled colony of their own, governing themselves and, unlike the other foreigners, not becoming Londoners. They paid for their many privileges by keeping Bishopsgate in repair. Their importance declined during the sixteenth century, and finally their privileges were withdrawn by Elizabeth. During the fourteenth century the great fleet of Venetian galleys that came each year to the north made London its port, bringing much trade and inducing the Londoners themselves to enter the Mediterranean, which they did with great success in the days of Whittington. The merchants who did this leagued themselves together in something of the manner of the Hansards, forming the

Merchant Adven-
turers of London
and from them
London's overseas
trade really began.
They started to-
wards the end of
the fourteenth cen-
tury as an offshoot
of the Mercers'
Company and set
up trading centres
in many parts of
Europe. Then
they began to push
out into the Medi-
terranean and, with
a Royal charter
that allowed them
to make commer-
cial treaties with
foreign princes, to

THE BANK OF ENGLAND

keep an armed force for the defence of their trade,
to make and enforce rules governing the conduct of
their members; they set up a European headquarters
at Bruges and later in Antwerp. The Greshams were
important members of the Company in Tudor times, and
it was whilst he was working at their house in Antwerp
that Sir Thomas Gresham learned how to conduct
business. It was there, too, that he saw the value of a
centre where all merchants could meet to carry on their
business. It was in its Bourse, or Exchange, that most
of the business of Antwerp was transacted; and Sir
Thomas decided that when he returned to his own
country London should have its Exchange too. So he
bought the site, gave the money, and an Exchange was
designed by a Flemish architect. Stow shows how much

the building was needed in his picture of Lombard Street:

"The merchants and tradesmen, as well English as strangers, for their general making of bargains, contracts and commerce, did usually meet twice every day. But these meetings were unpleasant and troublesome by reason of walking and talking in an open street, being there constrained to endure all extremes of weather or else to shelter themselves in shops."

As the building was in brick and the English were not yet skilled in this craft, many of the workmen came from Flanders and the English workmen gave a good deal of trouble, often going on strike because they had to work with foreigners. But at last the building was finished. For some time, however, Gresham had a great deal of difficulty in getting people to use it. The Exchange was built as an open courtyard round which was an arcade and above this were shops. The chief difficulty was getting these let. Gresham surmounted it by first getting the Queen to promise that she would open the Exchange, and then by offering to let the shops rent free for a year to any who would take them up and stock them before the opening.

All being prepared, [says Stow,] the Queen's Majesty, attended by her nobility, came from her house in the Strand called Somerset House, and entered the city through Temple Bar, through Cheap, and so by the north side of the Burse to Sir Thomas Gresham's house in Bishopsgate, where she dined. After dinner her Majesty, returning through Cornhill, entered the Burse on the south side, and after she had viewed every part thereof above ground, especially the Pawne, which was richly furnished with all sorts of the finest wares in the city, she caused the same Burse to be proclaimed by a herald of trumpets, the "Royal Exchange."

It soon became very popular and drew much trade to London.

The writings of the early seventeenth century are full of its glories.

How full of riches was that Royal Exchange, [says one writer of the time,] rich men in the midst of it, rich goods below. There men walked upon the top of a wealthy mine; considering what eastern treasures, costly spices and suchlike were laid up in the cellars of that place. As for the upper part of it, was it not the great store-house whence the nobility of England were furnished with all those costly things wherewith they did adorn either their houses or themselves.

The whole building was destroyed by the Great Fire, only the statue of the founder surviving. It was soon rebuilt but on a somewhat larger scale, and Addison gives us a fine description of the business that was done there in his time :

"There is no place in the town which I so much love to frequent as the Royal Exchange. It gives me a secret satisfaction, and in some measure gratifies my vanity as an Englishman, to see so rich an assembly of countrymen and foreigners consulting together upon the private business of mankind, and making this metropolis a kind of emporium for the whole earth. I must confess I look upon the High 'Change to be a great council in which all the considerable nations have their representatives. Factors in the trading world are what ambassadors are in the political world ; they negotiate affairs, conclude treaties and maintain a good correspondence between those wealthy societies of men which are divided from one another by seas and oceans. I have often been pleased to hear disputes adjusted between an inhabitant of Japan and an alderman of London ; or to see a subject of the Great Moghul entering a league with one of the Czar of Muscovy. . . . Our ships are laden with the harvest of every climate, our tables are filled with pyramids of china, and adorned with the workmanship of Japan ; our morning draught comes to us from the remotest corners of the earth ; we repair our bodies with the drugs of America, and repose ourselves under Indian canopies. . . . Our English merchant converts the tin of his own country into gold and exchanges his wool for rubies. The Mahometans are clothed with our British manufacture, and the inhabitants of the frozen zone with the fleeces of our sheep."

Such was the trade of London in the early part of the eighteenth century ; it had reached that level largely because of the facilities afforded by the Royal Exchange. This second building remained until 1838 when it was destroyed in its turn by fire, and once more, by a curious coincidence, only Gresham's statue survived. The Exchange was soon rebuilt on the same plan as before, but later the quadrangle was covered with a glass dome.

Since then a series of frescoes illustrating London history has been painted on the walls. The drapers' shops have gone, there are no longer stores of rich spices in the cellars and the chief business done is insurance, but the golden grasshopper, the badge of the Greshams, still sits above the building.

During the seventeenth century London's commerce really became world-wide. The risks of this greater trade could no longer be borne by single merchants acting alone or even by the Merchant Adventurers, and so associations of merchants were formed to carry on the new trades. All these new associations were formed on the lines of the Adventurers ; they were granted charters which gave each the monopoly rights in some branch of trade and certain rights of self-government which generally included the power to make commercial treaties with foreign princes and to control their servants, especially overseas. They were also " joint-stock " companies ; that is, the individual members found the money for carrying on the trade, they elected the governing body which managed the affairs of the company, and they shared in the profits ; but it was the company as a corporate body that did the actual trading, acting through its paid servants. This joint stock principle is very important, for out of it has grown all our modern commercial and industrial development. It meant that London's trade was no longer confined to a few wealthy men ; anyone with a little money, he need not even be a merchant, could take shares. In this way the interest in trading was spread over a wider class of people and very big enterprises could be built up.

One of the first of these companies was the Russia Company formed in 1553 to discover a North-East Passage and to open up trade with China by this route. It sent out Willoughby and Challoner with an expedition. Willoughby died in the Arctic but Challoner discovered the White Sea, visited Moscow and opened up trade with Russia and Persia. This company flourished until 1699 when it was dissolved, but its members still continued as an association of Russian merchants and this association still exists.

Several similar companies were formed during the reign of Elizabeth, some for trade in the Mediterranean, others for trade with the west coast of Africa, and then, in 1601, came the greatest of them all, the East India Company. After a few voyages the members decided to become a joint-stock company; and on this basis they traded with India and the East Indies until 1661, when Charles II granted them a charter allowing them to make treaties with native princes and to keep armed forces for the defence of their ships and their warehouses. From this time on the company began to build up an Indian Empire which was greatly increased through the conquests made by Robert Clive nearly a century later. Gradually it became a governing rather than a trading company and in 1833 its trading monopoly was ended and for the next twenty years it was the government of British India. It was finally dissolved in 1854 when its work was taken over by the India Office and placed under the control of a Secretary of State responsible to Parliament.

In the year after the Great Fire the company ordered its agent in China to buy and send home " One hundred pounds of the best tay you can gett," the first news we have of the introduction of tea into England. Some of this tea was drunk by Lady St. John in the Chinese Parlour of Old Battersea House, a house which may still be seen down by the river near Battersea Church. The offices of the company, where the whole of the government of India was carried on in addition to a vast trade, were in Leadenhall Street, and here Charles Lamb was employed as a clerk.

The Hudson's Bay Company is the only one of these great companies that still carries on trade. It was formed in 1670 with Prince Rupert as one of the governors, and it rapidly built up a trade with the Indians of North

M

America. It, too, controlled the government of vast territories, but the foundation of the United States of America restricted its area of trade and the growth of the Dominion of Canada deprived it of its control of the government of the north-west. Its offices are in Bishopsgate and it still carries on a very valuable trade in furs and other products of the Arctic and the regions around Hudson Bay.

Besides these there were several others, hardly trading concerns but of very great importance in the development of London's commerce and also to the history of England. These were the land and development companies that colonized Ulster and the English colonies on the coast of North America. It was they who founded our colonial Empire and nursed the infant settlements until they were old enough to stand alone. We shall see how they worked in a later chapter.

All this trade needed money, so that during the eighteenth century London became the great banking and financial centre that it is to-day. In the early times the Lombards, who had the sole right to collect the Pope's revenues in England, were the great bankers ; but after the Reformation, the London goldsmiths, many of them descendants of the Lombards, took their place. They took charge of their customers' money and kept current accounts ; their receipts were passed from hand to hand almost like bank notes, and the letters from their customers asking them to pay out some of the money did duty as cheques. A lot of the money in their possession was lent to merchants to finance their businesses and a great deal more was lent to the Government on the security of the revenue. No one minded this so long as the Government paid the interest and repaid the loans when they became due, but when the Governments of Charles II and James II failed to do this, the credit of the goldsmiths failed and they began to lose the confidence of their customers. Then came the Revolution, and the Government of William III was so insecure that it could not borrow money enough to carry on even for a few weeks until some of the revenue granted by Parliament was collected. It seemed as though we must have another revolution, but William Paterson, a Scotsman, with the help of a number of London merchants, got together a fund of over a million pounds which they agreed to lend to the Government for ever in return for an annual payment of one hundred thousand pounds and certain monopoly rights. They were to become a Chartered Company known as the " Governour and Company of the Bank of England," and they were given the sole right to manufacture money out of nothing but the national credit, by printing bank-notes up to the value of the money they had lent to the Government. In addition to this they could also print notes to the value of any securities such as land or gold held by them. As money is really only credit—that is, its value depends on whether we have actually done a certain amount of work to produce goods or whether people believe that we will keep our word when we promise to do such work—this making of money is quite all right. It only goes wrong when we print, or coin, more money than our work and what it produces is worth. Then, as there is nothing solid behind this extra money, it is worthless ; so the more of it we make the more expensive things become, and sooner or later the country goes bankrupt. This power of printing money is a very important one, and has a great deal to do with the pros-perity of England as well as of London. It is rather difficult to understand but we ought to try to do so because the future of our city depends so much on it.

The Bank of England is now the only body in England that can make money in this way, for even the Royal Mint only manufactures coins to sell to the Bank, so it cannot issue more than the Bank will buy. The Bank's own money is in the form of notes and you are all familiar with those for £1 and 10s. Now look at one and you will see that it says : " Bank of England Promise to pay the Bearer on Demand the sum of ONE POUND " ; so it is not really money, but only a promise to do something, and that promise is not worth the paper it is printed on unless people know that we will keep it by doing enough work to make it represent one pound's worth of goods. Therefore all that the Bank does is to put down on paper our promise to grow or make things, and then to enable us to use that credit as money for the purchase of goods. If the Bank restricts its note issue to an amount equal to the value of the work we have done, together with a further amount equal to the work people believe we will do, then our credit is good and we are prosperous. But if it goes beyond this then we suffer from what is called " inflation " ; we have promised to pay for more goods than we are able or willing to make so that the value of goods expressed in £ s. d. goes up. The Bank can step in and stop this by refusing to print more notes than we are really worth, but by printing in advance of the work we are actually going to do it can enable our factories to produce and our merchants to trade, and, as it is not a Government department, it can do this without fearing trouble from political parties. The Bank of England, however, does not deal directly with us except to cash its own notes or to sell us Government stocks. What we do is to use bank-notes as money and we don't worry about whether the Bank can cash them or not because we believe that it always will. But this was not always so. At first the Bank had a hard fight to get people to believe in it, and it had many rivals, especially the goldsmiths, who tried to ruin it by buying up its notes and then presenting them all at the same time. They failed, and gradually people came to believe in the Bank—that is, in the honesty of the London merchants and the British people who were behind it.

In time other banks grew up and it is with these that we generally deal. They, however, cannot print notes— that is, they cannot create credit. All they can do is to keep our accounts for us, and enable us to pay our debts quickly and easily by means of cheques. They also keep money moving and so we are able to live with fewer notes and coins in circulation than we should want if there were no banks. The banks keep their accounts with the Bank of England which in this way knows pretty well how much we are worth, and so can keep steady the amount of money in circulation, calling in notes if there are too many in use and printing more if there are not enough.

This only works within the country, because it is only there that bank-notes can be made " legal tender "—that is, the seller can be compelled to accept them in payment for his goods. For foreign trade some other method must be used because the foreign merchant cannot be compelled to accept Bank of England notes and some system of exchange must be found that he will accept. Many such systems have been used : cowrie shells in West Africa, coiled baskets in Alaska, Chinese bronze jars in Borneo, but none has been found to equal gold. There are many reasons for this but perhaps the best one is that the merchant (or country) taking gold for its goods knows just how much other goods it can get in exchange, or to put it in another way, just what any other currency is worth when changed into its own. This of course is true only when the gold is used ; if it is just locked up somewhere, as the United States of America did with it before the war, it becomes of no value at all.

To be of any use for trade gold must be circulated. To do this, when there is not enough of it to pay for all the goods that are wanted, or for all the promises to pay that are likely to be presented, some system of international banking has to be discovered so that the bills drawn on the merchants of one country by those of another can be used to purchase goods in much the same way that we use bank-notes. It was in London that this system of bills of exchange was developed so that it could be used in modern world trade. London was able to do this very largely because the actual working of the Bank of England was free from the control of the Government. The Bank works within the powers given it by Parliament, but it is not owned by the State as are the central banks of other countries. So no matter what kind of government may be in power, foreign merchants know that it cannot use the Bank of England for political purposes, and that, because of this freedom, bills drawn on London will always carry something very near their face value and will not change very much on account of political changes in the country. This is a different side of the Bank's business from that of managing the internal currency of the country ; but I have tried to explain it as simply as I could because so much of our national prosperity depends on it, and because so many of you will have to use it when you work " in the city." During the eighteenth century trade increased so much that it was impossible for any one person or even for a small group of people to find all the money needed to start a new factory, build a railway or run a line of steamships, so that a new plan had to be found. The idea hit upon was to issue a large number of shares each representing some small sum of money such as a pound or even a shilling. People subscribed for these and thus provided the money. If the credit of the company were good, or it was earning a lot of money and paying a high rate of interest, people were willing to pay much more than the face value of the shares in order to get them ; but, if its earnings were poor, then the shares cost less than their nominal value. So there was a regular market in shares. In the early days anyone could deal in shares, and there was no control over the dealers, a state of affairs that led to much wild speculation, and eventually to the South Sea Bubble which you will have read about in your history books. In order to protect both them- selves and their customers against dishonest dealers, the leading stock brokers formed a society which made rules for controlling the business. As only honest dealers were allowed to join this society people came to trust its members and they were able to control the whole trade. At first the members met at Lloyd's Coffee House or at the Royal Exchange, but their business soon became too great for these quarters and so they built for themselves the London Stock Exchange, where they still meet for business.

The other great financial business of which London is the centre is insurance. This began with merchants covering themselves against losses by paying into a common fund, out of which their individual losses were met, and there is still a certain amount of this mutual insurance carried on. Then, after the terrible losses caused by the Great Fire, citizens began to cover themselves against this risk too, and companies were formed, not of the merchants themselves but of men who made this insurance their whole business. At first only mercantile and fire losses were covered and the companies specialized, some taking only commercial risks, others covering only fire. But gradually other risks of loss were covered in this way and to-day one can insure against any loss, even that of one's birthday party being spoiled by rain. There are many famous insurance companies in London, some of them taking life insurance, some fire, and some covering other risks. But perhaps the most famous of them all is Lloyd's.

The founder was Edward Lloyd, who kept a coffee house where the merchants, ship-owners and sea-captains used to meet. For the convenience of his customers Lloyd used to issue a newsletter containing information about ships and other matters of interest, and from this has grown *Lloyd's List and Shipping Gazette*, which, with the exception of the official *London Gazette*, is the oldest newspaper in England. In 1770 those of Lloyd's customers who were specially interested in insurance, moved to the Royal Exchange and founded the Society of Lloyd's Underwriters, which exists to-day. It now has magnificent premises of its own in Leadenhall Street.

THE MAIN ENTRANCE TO LLOYD'S BUILDING, LEADENHALL STREET

The main interest of Lloyd's is still marine insurance and it has its own staff of inspectors who are sent to examine ships, both new ones before they leave the builders' hands and those already in service. "Classed A 1 at Lloyds" is still the mark of a first-class ship and the ships of all nations are insured by the underwriters of this corporation.

But the members deal in all kinds of risk besides those to ships and their cargoes; they are willing to take a premium for the cover of almost any kind of loss in any part of the world, their premiums being high or low according to whether they think the risk of their having to pay out the amount insured is great or small. When they have taken up a risk it is shared in agreed proportions amongst several of the members, who thus cover themselves against having to pay out more than they can afford.

There are many other insurance companies in London, and in other places as well. For an annual payment these will undertake to insure against loss of life, of goods, of houses, of motor-cars and of many other things. They will pay you an annual sum when you reach a certain age and cover you against loss by accident to yourself or other people. Indeed almost any risk that is not too great can be insured against. The companies, however, usually take care to insure themselves against loss by reinsuring with Lloyd's underwriters, so that when you take out an insurance policy it is usually a group of Lloyd's members who will really pay you should you suffer the loss against which you have insured.

There are many other financial affairs that are carried on in London besides banking and insurance. There is dealing in foreign currencies and in gold and precious metals; the buying, at discount, of commercial bills and other promises to pay; the buying and selling of property in all parts of the world. A whole book might be written about them. Together they form the London Money

Market and make the city the leading financial centre in the world. Much of this leading position is due to the foresight of Sir Thomas Gresham, and his crest of the golden grasshopper might well become the badge of all those engaged in finance in London.

DICKENS' HOUSE

CHAPTER XI

HOW LONDON IS GOVERNED

LONDON is the largest and the busiest city in the world. There are nearly four million people living in the County of London, and another four and a half millions in Greater London. There are thousands of miles of streets to be looked after; hundreds of thousands of cars, lorries, buses and carts to be controlled; drains and water supply, roads and bridges, education and public health, and many other matters to be dealt with: problems far more difficult to solve than those that the governments of many independent countries have to face. Someone has to govern this great city and to solve its problems. Who is it? Well, there is a considerable number of authorities concerned, for, strange as it may seem, London as a whole has no central government of its own, but is looked after by a large number of different governments.

London is a part of the United Kingdom, so that many of its laws are made by Parliament and enforced by various Government departments, each of which has at its head a Minister who is responsible to Parliament. The people of London elect their Members of Parliament, and these, together with those representing the rest of the country, pass the laws. Most of these laws apply to the whole of the country, so that this is quite a fair arrangement; but some of them affect the London area only. It is quite possible (and sometimes it happens) that some very necessary, and even urgent, London matter gets held up, either because the members for the rest of the country cannot see its importance to London, or because Parliament is too busy with national affairs to give to this special legislation the attention that it deserves. The London area is so large, its importance as the metropolis and as a commercial and industrial area is so great, it has so many people (nearly a quarter of the whole population of Great Britain lives in the London area), that its problems are often of a different kind from those of the rest of the country and need special attention. Yet, unlike all the other large towns of Britain, the London area has no authority in control of the whole. Its various parts have councils of one sort or another, but, apart from Parliament, there is no one body of people responsible for the government of the whole of the Metropolitan area.

The various councils and other bodies have a great variety of powers and rule over very different districts.

At the centre there is the ancient Corporation of the City of London, one of the oldest, and in many ways the most independent and important local government in the whole country. It has very great powers, and in some respects is almost independent of Parliament, but it rules only over the square mile of the ancient city, which to-day has the smallest resident population of any part of the London area. Around it are the twenty-seven metropolitan boroughs, each with its mayor, aldermen and councillors, its town clerk and other officials. These are all within the County of London and are, to some extent, controlled by the London County Council. This is inner London, a district which, when it was formed in 1889, was separated from the surrounding villages and small towns by a belt of open country. Now these surrounding villages have grown until they touch one another and have reached to the county boundary. So inner London is enclosed within a ring of metropolitan boroughs, county boroughs, urban and even rural districts each with its own council. Their people work in London; their problems are those of the London area; they are really part of London; yet they are not treated as forming part of the Capital but as belonging to one or other of the rural counties in which they were once villages. Besides the elected bodies there are others whose members are appointed by various authorities. There are the Metropolitan Police, controlled by the Home Office; the Post Office, which is a Government department; the Metropolitan Water Board which controls the water supply over a great part of the area; the London Passenger Transport Board controlling all the road passenger transport within the London area and running coaches to places fifty or more miles away; and the Port of London Authority controlling all the docks (but not the riverside wharves) and the river traffic from Brentford right down to the Nore.

If we tried to describe the work of all these different authorities we should need a whole book, and when it was written it would be a description, not of the local governments of the London district, but of the whole system of local government throughout the country. So here we will think only about the various bodies within the County of London; but do not forget all the others just outside, for they too are concerned with the problems of London's government, problems such as no other place in the world has to solve. Some people think that the difficulties will never be cleared up until the whole of the London area, both the county and the districts around, has been placed under one supreme London government.

Why is there all this confusion in London's government? The reason is simply that London was never made—like Topsy, it just grew—and to-day that growth has got it to the stage when it is rather confused. To understand that confusion and to plan for the improvement of London's government in the future we must understand how it has grown. We must study its history. So let us get back to the beginning and trace the growth of London's government from early times to the present day.

We need not go back to the very early times, or even to Roman days. Roman London had a local government, as had every other Roman town, but that government disappeared during the confused period of the English conquest, when London itself vanished from recorded history. Some scholars think that they can trace remains of the Roman government in some of the forms of the city's government to-day, but this is very doubtful. If there are any remains of Roman institutions to be found in the government of modern London they are as deeply buried as are the remains of the houses and pavements, and are far more difficult to discover.

The city of London as we know it is a town of the English after they had become Christian, and it was then governed in exactly the same way as any other group of English families was governed. For the English were not townsmen as the Romans and the Britons were. They avoided towns and preferred to settle in hamlets and villages ; a family, or at most a small group of kindred families living together, was ruled by a headman acting with the help of the older men of the group. These family groups were connected into larger ones called hundreds, and these again in later times into small kingdoms, which by the eighth century were gradually forming the greater kingdoms of later Saxon history. There are plenty of traces of this form of organization, not only in the London area, which is full of English villages, but within the walled city that had been Roman London. There are still the wards, each with its alderman, who together form the highest court in the city, and there are traces of the smaller groups to be seen in the organization of the early Norman city. But London was a port, with many foreign traders who needed keeping under some sort of control, so in very early times we find there was a port-reeve. We do not know what his exact duties were, but we may guess that they included some control over the foreign merchants, perhaps the collecting of port dues and the regulation of the shipping. When Wessex conquered the whole country and London became one of Alfred's key fortresses against the Danes, the port-reeve may have

COUNTY HALL, FROM THE RIVER

acted as its chief magistrate ; but it is possible that Alfred gave it an earldorman, as he did his other burghs, or fortified places. We do not know for certain, but in any case you must be careful not to confuse this officer with an alderman. In Danish times a new body appeared, the Court of Husting, and a new officer, the staller, who seems to have been some sort of military officer ; for it was Ansgar the Staller who led the London men at the battle of Hastings. The staller has disappeared, but the Court of Husting still exists and has some very important work to do in the government of the city. In fact most of the old forms of London government still exist in the city, for London has always preferred the way of evolution to that of revolution. The old bodies have been kept in existence but their duties have gradually been altered to suit new conditions. London prefers to adapt old institutions rather than to create new ones, though she is quite ready to do even this should it be necessary. So the reeve has gone, but his duties are performed by the court of aldermen and the Lord Mayor : the staller has vanished, but there are now the two sheriffs who may still be carrying on some of his work, and the Lord Mayor combines the duties of the old English king with those of the earldorman of Alfred's time, carrying the sceptre and the uplifted sword as signs of his kingship within the city of London.

When the Normans came they had to allow this old government to continue ; they were not strong enough to alter it. They tried to get control by appointing a sheriff (who was a Royal officer) whose duties included the collection of taxes, seeing that criminals were tried and punished, and getting the Royal will obeyed. In London the citizens were all free men ; there were no serfs or villains ; but the city as a whole was not yet free, although her great size, the number and discipline of her men and the warlike reputation of her citizens made even the powerful Norman kings treat her with

great respect. So long as the sheriff was appointed by
the King, London was not a free city, so that the first
thing the citizens did was to work for the right to appoint
the sheriff themselves. This they did in a typically
London way. Taking advantage of the need of Henry I
for ready money they bought from him the right to
appoint not only the sheriff of London but his colleague
of Middlesex as well, thus securing themselves from
any future dispute as to whether London was in Middlesex or not. Now what had been granted by the King
might be taken away, but what had been bought and
paid for by an annual rent could never be taken back
so long as the rent was paid, and London was far too
powerful for this right ever to be cancelled by force.
Now London was a free city owing nothing to the King
but a general allegiance and a small annual payment that
could never be increased. So far as her internal government was concerned she could grow in her own way
without any interference from the King. When some
new form of government seemed to be needed the city's
method was to work out the new idea, put it into practice, and then get the King to recognize the change by
a charter. Thus changes came about slowly, each
being grafted on to some older form in much the same
way as a gardener grafts new shoots on to an older plant.

It was in this way that London got her Mayor. At
the end of the twelfth century many French towns were
setting up communes, that is, self-governments, and
as many Londoners were also citizens of these French
towns they knew all about this new idea and thought that
it was a good one. With a commune London would be
able to make its own laws as well as to tax itself and
control its own trade as it was already doing. The
French towns were getting their rights from their over-
lords, but London had no overlord of the usual kind,
and to ask the King for a charter would be to admit
that he had rights over the city. So London did not
ask anyone if it might have a Mayor, it just elected one

and said nothing about the commune. Then, in 1191, came the chance of securing from the King the acknowledgement that the Londoners had the right to elect a Mayor. Richard Lionheart was in an Austrian prison and money was needed for his ransom. A bargain was struck with Prince John, the Regent; London would find the money in return for a charter recognizing that the Mayor was the chief magistrate of the city. He was to be elected by the citizens themselves without any interference from the King, but was to present himself before the King or his officers immediately after his election and to take the oath of allegiance. Nothing was said about an annual election and the first Mayor, Henry Fitz-Alwyn, held office for several years : only later did the election become an annual one, and then only because the citizens found that it was better for them to change their chief magistrate every year.

But by setting up its commune London did not introduce any new form of government. Sheriffs, aldermen, Folkmote and Court of Husting still went on doing their work ; only now they were all under the control of the Mayor and his council representing the city as a whole. That is what London has always done. She has never scrapped her old government and invented a new one ; she has just altered the old one sufficiently to make it work well under new conditions, and the government of Great Britain and the Commonwealth has developed in the same way. Following the example of London we have never made a complete and violent change in our forms of government ; only once, in the time of Cromwell, did we even try, and then it was a failure and we had to go back to the old way of gradual change. We have either grafted something new on to the old, or we have given some existing form some new powers, not much, just sufficient to make it work well under new conditions. That is why the British system of democracy is so strong to-day ; but we need to study our history, for unless we do we cannot understand how we have

become what we are, and unless we do understand this
we cannot make wise changes for the future.

This introduction of a Mayor did not make much
difference at first, but the citizens were very quick to
see that whoever elected the Mayor really ruled the
city. At first this power lay in the hands of the great
merchants, many of whom were of foreign origin.
They probably introduced the commune because they
saw that the old form of government would very likely
fall into the hands of the craftsmen, who were far more
numerous and were now beginning to organize themselves into guilds. But the craftsmen saw the value
of the new form of government too, and began to try to
get into control. For a hundred years this struggle went
on; it even influenced the struggle that was going on
between the King and his barons all through the
thirteenth century. Sometimes in London, as in the
country, there was bloodshed; sometimes those who
wanted change were too impatient to wait for the change
to come naturally but wanted to make a new world
suddenly. In the end changes were made slowly,
and by the close of the century the city was governed by
a Mayor (usually elected by whatever happened to be the
most powerful class at the time), assisted by a council
elected by the whole body of citizens. This council,
together with the aldermen, made the laws for the city;
whilst the actual government was carried out by the
Mayor and aldermen acting as a court of justice. Its
powers have been changed from time to time, but ever
since the days of Edward I this has been the form of
the city's government, as it is to-day.

By the beginning of the fourteenth century the citizens
were divided into three classes : the wealthy landowners,
who were often barons with estates in the country, as
well as being London citizens ; the merchants, many
of whom were of foreign origin; and the craftsmen.
Gradually the two first classes merged into one whilst
the craftsmen split into two, the skilled men, organized

into guilds, and the unskilled men and labourers. These last, however, were freemen of the city, for there were no unfree in London. There were differences of ability and intelligence, of education and skill, of wealth and power, but all London citizens were equal before the law and all had their rights in the government of their city. London in the fourteenth century was a democracy, perhaps the first real democracy to exist in this world.

During this century, too, the craft guilds became powerful, and by the time of the Peasants' Revolt they were in control of the city's government. Almost at once the guilds began to split into two groups. The craft guilds such as the Drapers, the Mercers, the Goldsmiths and a number of less wealthy ones were opposed by the Fishmongers, the Grocers and others whose trade was to supply food. The craft guilds wanted cheap food and cheap raw materials ; they did not much care where these things came from so long as they were cheap and plentiful. The victuallers, however, wanted to keep these things under their control. It is the old story of free trade and protection that takes up so much of our history during the nineteenth century, being fought out four hundred years earlier on the smaller stage of London. It got itself mixed up with the Wars of the Roses as well as with the Peasants' Revolt, and was not really settled until Tudor times.

By the end of the fourteenth century the right to elect the Mayor had been given to Common Hall, a court which was supposed to be a general meeting of all the citizens, but in practice was confined to the members of the guilds, whilst the Common Council was elected by the citizens of the wards. In 1475, however, it was decided that Common Hall should consist of the Mayor, Aldermen and Common Council, together with the liverymen of the guilds. These were the more important and wealthy members of the guilds who formed a sort of governing committee. Common Hall was to choose the Mayor and certain other officials, but the

THE GUILDHALL LIBRARY

citizens had the right to be present at the election. To-day the Lord Mayor is elected by Common Hall, the aldermen first choosing three candidates from those aldermen who have served in the office of sheriff. These three are then presented to Common Hall which elects one as Lord Mayor. The alderman so elected is then presented to all those present in Guildhall and is said to have been chosen in the presence of "a tumultuous multitude of citizens," which represents the general assembly of the early days.

By the fifteenth century the Mayor had become a person of very great importance, ranking next to the King whenever His Majesty visited the city, and always careful to preserve the rights, liberties, and prestige of the city. When he attended before the Royal Courts to take the oath of allegiance he was accompanied by all the principal citizens as well as by the officials, and out of this there grew the Lord Mayor's Show, a pageant in which each of the guilds vied with the others in putting on the most attractive feature.

Some of these Mayors (by the middle of the sixteenth century they are always called Lord Mayors), were very famous men, leading the city's fleets and armies during the Hundred Years' War, and entertaining kings and great lords, both English and foreign. Perhaps the most famous is Richard Whittington, the Dick Whittington of the fairy tale, who was four times Mayor during the fifteenth century. He was far from being the poor boy that the legend makes him out to have been, for his father was a Gloucestershire knight and he married the daughter of another wealthy west-country gentleman. He may have travelled up to London by the carrier's waggon; he would have been a boy of about eight years old then, and as there were no coaches in those days he must have come in some sort of waggon, for a boy of that age could hardly have ridden from Gloucestershire to London. He was apprenticed to Sir John Fitzwarren, a Merchant Adventurer, but this was quite a usual thing, for many of the younger sons of country gentlemen were entering trade at that time, not only in London but in Bristol and other places as well. He prospered in his trade of mercer, and seems, like other members of his craft, to have been interested in the Merchant Adventurers who were then pushing English trade into the Mediterranean. According to the legend it was in a venture to Algiers that Whittington laid the foundations of his fortune ; and the legend may thus far be true, with the " cat " as a ship rather than an animal, although there is an actual cat figured in one of the Whittington coats of arms.

Whittington lent money to the Government during the Agincourt campaign and he would certainly have entertained the King on his visit to London, for Whittington had been Mayor for the third time in 1406 and was to hold the office again in 1419. He was never knighted and there is no reason for believing the story that he burned several thousand pounds worth of war loan after a banquet to the King. He was far too good a business man to waste money in that way. He was a liberal benefactor to the poor, as were all wealthy men in those days ; but he was a far more liberal benefactor to the city, for he left money for the rebuilding of Guildhall, he helped the Mercers' School, he founded a library at the Greyfriars and another at the Guildhall. With his friend John Carpenter, the town clerk, he founded the City of London School and he left money for almshouses and other charitable purposes in the city.

The actual duties of the city government at this time were very different from those of its successor to-day. They were concerned with the regulation of trade, the prices and quality of goods sold in the markets and shops, with the control of foreign merchants, with the details of the nightly watch supposed to be kept by the citizens of each ward ; but with the thousand and one matters that concern a modern town council they did not trouble at all.

During Tudor and Stuart times the form of government in the city remained unaltered, but there were several important changes in its duties. Attempts were made, without much success, to keep the streets clean and in some sort of repair ; some effort was made to control building ; the severe outbreaks of the Plague made it necessary for the authorities to look after public health and the increase of the population compelled them to improve the water supply. These matters were usually left until it was almost too late to do anything, and when regulations were made it was very difficult to get them carried out.

The greatest change was that brought about by the Poor Law of Elizabeth. No longer was the care of the poor left entirely to the Church and to private charity ; it became the duty of the public authorities, and the money was to be provided from a rate levied on all householders.

But for the most part the energies of the Corporation were directed to preserving their liberties against the Stuart Kings who were trying to set up a strong central government and who found London very much in their way. Although there was a strong Royalist party in London, the citizens as a whole were against the King, and by supporting the Parliament they managed to keep their privileged position. In some ways this was unfortunate because it led them to refuse to take advantage of the opportunity for setting up some control over the Greater London that was growing up outside their walls. Several suggestions were made for increasing the size of the city, but the citizens opposed them all because any extension of their city would be the subject of an Act of Parliament, and they were afraid that this might mean some outside control of their internal affairs. Consequently, as the built-up area increased, various other local authorities were formed, often with overlapping powers ; by the end of the eighteenth century the government of the London area outside the city was in a hopeless muddle which we have not cleared up yet.

As the population of the city declined, so did the activities of the Corporation. It still did a great deal in the fight for freedom, as we have already seen, but as a local government its activities almost stopped. The State had failed to control it, and so the State left it alone ; and, like all human institutions when they are left alone, it went to sleep.

The new London around the city was growing rapidly, but its governments were still those of country villages with powers quite unsuited to the management of places whose populations were growing rapidly. Except for the city of Westminster, which was ruled by a committee appointed by the Dean of the Abbey and the chief house-holders, the area outside of the city of London had two sets of controllers. First there were the country justices of the peace who were responsible for punishing petty offenders, fixing the price of bread and the rates of wages, and doing a number of other odd jobs placed upon them by Parliament. They were not paid for all this work but the Privy Council did keep them under some sort of control. Next there were the parish officers, some appointed by the justices and others by the annual meeting of parishioners called the Easter Vestry. In the Middle Ages the government of the villages had been carried on by the manorial courts, but after the Reformation much of their work was passed on to the church officials, the churchwardens and their assistants, who were appointed by the parish at its Easter Vestry meeting. To these the Elizabethan Poor Law added the overseers who had charge of the Poor Law administration. These too were appointed by the Vestry, but were controlled by the justices and their duties were constantly being increased by Acts of Parliament. The churchwardens and overseers appointed the constable and other parish officials ; they saw that the ordinary punishments of whipping, setting in the stocks or the ducking stool were carried out by the constable; they appointed officials to round up stray cattle; they gave out gifts of clothing or money to help eke out scanty wages; they apprenticed boys and girls, and they settled small disputes amongst the villagers.

In all this work they had the support of the justices, before whom they could bring any person who was accused or suspected of small crimes. The justice heard the case and then either ordered some slight punishment to be administered immediately, or committed the accused for trial before the quarterly meeting of all the justices of the county or before one of the King's judges at the assizes.

Whilst the villages were small these officials could look after them quite easily, but as they grew and became part of a town, it was found that the parish officers and the justices could no longer do all the work. So Parliament set up special boards of commissioners to do certain jobs. Paving Commissioners were appointed to look after the paving and repair of certain streets; Highways Commissioners to make new main roads and to keep them in repair; Sewerage Commissioners to look after the drains, and so on. By the beginning of the nineteenth century there were nearly three hundred of these boards in London, yet very little was being done; for once they were appointed there was no one to look after them or to see that they carried out their duties. Although some of them were efficient, others did nothing at all except to levy a rate, out of which they paid themselves. In the city there was the Corporation; outside, each parish had its Vestry; there were numbers of boards of one sort or another and there were the county justices, but there was no central authority with any sort of control over the whole area that was rapidly being built over. There was not even anyone except the parish constables and their watch to keep the peace and arrest criminals.

This, in fact, was the first matter that had to be taken

St. Marylebone Town Hall

in hand, for in the days of distress that followed the Napoleonic Wars mobs of hungry men were forming and they were a great danger. The first reform therefore was that of the police. In 1829 Parliament set up the Metropolitan Police Force, a body of disciplined men under the direct control of the Home Secretary, and responsible to him for keeping order. It was difficult to decide the area over which they should have control, but at last it was determined that they should control all the parishes that came within a radius of twelve miles of Charing Cross. The distance was made twelve miles because in the old days the King's Provost Marshal had always been in control of an area extending to that distance from wherever the King happened to be. When the Government had become settled this official's headquarters had been established in New Scotland Yard, part of the old Palace of Whitehall, and as the new Commissioner took over his duties and his headquarters it was decided that he should have control over that radius.

There were two problems to solve before anything else could be done to set up a real common government for the London area. The first was to settle just how large the area was to be, and the second to decide what sort of body was to control it. Had the City Corporation been willing to take over a larger area both problems might have been settled at once. The Corporation however refused to do this, so that nothing was done except to increase the powers of some of the Vestries, to unite some of the parishes under Boards of Guardians for Poor Law work, and to set up a number of Sewerage Commissions.

These reforms carried the people on to the middle oi the century, when the state of the river made it necessary to make further changes. The result was the creation of the Metropolitan Board of Works, a body of men who were to take over the management of main roads and their bridges, main drainage, and other matters that concerned the whole of the London area. It was, however, given a much smaller district than that of the police. At about the same time the Boards of Guardians within this area were placed under the general control of the Metropolitan Asylums Board. Finally, in 1870, there came the London Schools Board. This was an elected body which had to provide elementary schools in all those districts that came within the area of the Board of Works, and where the number of school places already existing was not sufficient for the number of children of school age. The School Board, however, had no control over the very large number of Church schools that were already working in the various parishes. The city retained its independence, but the Board of Works and the London Schools Board had some duties to do even there.

At last, in 1889, it was felt that the time had come when some real unified government should be given to London as a whole. There were far too many authorities with overlapping duties, and people were beginning to feel that there should be an elected body, on the lines of the new county councils, in place of the Board of Works. The Vestries and the Boards of Guardians were left alone to carry out their local duties; the Asylums Board and the Schools Board were still left in charge of their own special tasks; but the whole area under the Board of Works was made into an administrative county and given a county council of its own. To this council there was given the duties of the Board of Works and some of the duties carried by the other county councils of the country. Something had been done at last to give London a real unity of government, but much of the good work was undone soon after, when the Vestries were abolished, and in their places there were set up twenty-seven metropolitan boroughs, each with its own council, mayor and aldermen. The idea was to give to the densely populated districts something of the dignity of the great county boroughs that existed throughout the country, but one important fact was overlooked.

These county boroughs were separated from each other by wide areas of country-side and the councils of the counties in which they were situated were mainly concerned with rural areas, so that their duties did not interfere much with each other. But in London the boroughs were not units in a county; they were part of the county, and no one, except the officials with their maps, could say where one borough ended and the next began; their boundaries in fact were marked on the map but the built-up areas were continuous. So this creation of the boroughs accentuated the differences of the parts rather than promoted the unity of the whole. At first there was considerable friction and jealousy between the boroughs and the county council, but much of this has died down as the various authorities found that they had to work together, and particularly since there has grown up a body of paid officials, both in the county council and in the borough councils. These officials have a high sense of public duty and a feeling that it is far better for them to work together for the public good than to quarrel over matters of local dignity. But the disunity remains and it is still sometimes so strong that necessary reforms have to be postponed. Unfortunately too, the unity of London has been further weakened by the setting up of such bodies as the Metropolitan Water Board, the Port of London Authority and the London Passenger Transport Board. As these bodies are not elected, some people maintain that they are not democratic, but each has done, and is still doing, fine work for London. Since the beginning of the present century something has been done to promote the unity of London by placing all forms of education (except the provision of libraries) under the county council, and by giving that body control of the Poor Law administration and of the wider aspects of public health control, such as the provision of hospitals.

The borough councils are responsible for matters of purely local concern. They look after the streets and

L.C.C. Estate at Peckham Rye

the local drains ; their medical officers of health and the sanitary inspectors who work under them are concerned with the health of the public, and in some boroughs there are clinics and dispensaries run by them, although they may not have hospitals. They maintain libraries and may arrange for lectures to be given at them, but they have no control over any kind of school or other educational institution. Some of them own electricity works and they may provide small parks and open spaces, although all the larger parks, with the exception of the Royal parks, are controlled by the county council. The borough councils may build houses or blocks of flats for working people, but so also may the L.C.C., and most of the boroughs are content to leave this duty to the central body. They levy rates for county and police purposes, but the Water Board levies and collects its own rates separately. They are still to a large extent independent of the county council and may even block its schemes for improvement, although here the common sense of the officials usually finds some compromise before much harm has been done. The boroughs too are handicapped by the fact that those in most need of improvements are those whose rates are highest and whose rateable value is lowest, so that they have the least money to spend. Something is done through the Equalization of Rates Fund, by which the richer boroughs help the poorest, but this is not nearly enough and the poor boroughs are still unable to carry out many necessary improvements because they cannot afford them.

We still, however, have not decided how big London ought to be, or what should be the relation between the county and that big area just outside whose people work in London but whose local affairs are administered by their own borough and county councils, whose interests are rural rather than metropolitan.

After the War, when there are so many new plans to be made, especially for the rebuilding of London and the

BUCKINGHAM PALACE FROM ST. JAMES'S PARK

remaking of its roads, all these various bodies will have to work together or they will get nothing done, and it may be found that before any successful plan can be put into operation some new area will have to be defined as London and some new authority set up to govern it. This is one of the problems that you will help to solve, and it will be an easier task now that you have learned something of the way in which London's government has grown up and how it works.

CHAPTER XII

LONDON THE LEADER

IN August, 1940, when the Luftwaffe tried to open Britain to invasion the main attack was aimed at London; and when the first attempt failed and the enemy changed over to night bombing it was London that got the heaviest attacks. Other British cities were severely damaged, but night after night for nine months London was hammered, losing hundreds of thousands of houses and suffering severe casualties. Eighty out of every hundred victims of the German bombs were Londoners. Her docks were destroyed by fire, her beautiful churches were laid in ruins, her traffic was disorganized. For nine months bombs were rained down, not on military objectives but on the densely packed industrial districts where the workers lived. The plan was to do so much damage and to kill and injure so many people that the survivors would force the Government to make peace. The same thing happened in 1944. Hitler's reply to the invasion of Normandy was to launch his flying bombs against London. Once again houses in the industrial areas were destroyed and ordinary citizens, men, women and children, were killed. But again the attempt failed. Londoners went calmly about their business, no demands were made for the diversion of forces for their defence, and by the end of August the attack had failed, beaten by the splendid courage of the ordinary Londoner quite as much as by the skill of the airmen, gunners and balloon men, and the bravery of the soldiers in Normandy.

Why did Hitler make these concentrated attacks on London? It was because he knew that London was the real leader in the fight for freedom; he believed that if he could once defeat London the conquest of the world would be easy. But London was not defeated. She fought back, her people showing that magnificent courage, resourcefulness and good humour that has distinguished the Cockney for hundreds of years. Time and time again London has led : in war, in the fight for political freedom and for liberty of thought; in commerce, in literature and in the arts. Her leadership in the Second World War was but the latest of these efforts.

Why London should have this gift of leadership it is hard to say. Perhaps it is because the people of a great trading centre need just those qualities of resource and initiative that make a leader ; perhaps it is because London draws to herself all that is best from all parts of the world, perhaps. . . . But we do not know. All we can say is that London has been a leader for many centuries, that her gifts of leadership have not deserted her in our own days. Possibly the real answer is that given by Dr. Johnson when he said : " In London a man may store his mind better than anywhere else ; nor does any place cure a man so well of arrogance or vanity, for there he will meet many who are his equals and some who are his superiors."

Let us look first at London as a leader in war. We will begin with the Navy. A complete history of the Royal Navy could be written from the records of London alone, but it would be quite impossible to write one and to leave London out. From the time of Alfred the Great, right down to the days of Henry VIII, London was one of the principal places from which war fleets were drawn and manned, and the Londoners often sent out a fleet to clear the North Sea of pirates when the rest of the country was at peace. They did this several times during the Danish invasions, but perhaps the most notable occasion was in the reign of Edward III, when the fleet of a Scottish pirate was plundering in the North Sea. As the King seemed unable to do anything the city sent out a fleet, commanded by Alderman Philpot, who engaged the enemy off the coast of Essex and destroyed his fleet. It was about this time, too, that the Londoners, again under the command of an alder-

o*

man, did such good work at the Battle of Sluys. The London ships were handled as an independent squadron and came on in such a way as to show that the men and their officers were well trained in naval fighting.

When the Royal Navy was begun by Henry VIII the chief dockyards were at Deptford and Woolwich, both in the London area; and from then, right down to the middle of the nineteenth century, the principal ships of the Navy were built on the Thames.

When we were at war it was the custom to strengthen the Royal Navy by adding ships borrowed from the seaports, and in fact the bulk of the fleets that defeated the Armada in 1588 consisted of such ships. London sent by far the greater number but she did something more. The English battle fleet consisted of eighty great ships, and of these no fewer than twenty were supplied by the city of London; twenty ships that were in no way inferior to the best of the Queen's ships in either size, sailing quality, or fire-power. Under the Stuarts this custom of borrowing ships from the ports was given up; but only after a long struggle, the famous Ship-money dispute, in which London took the lead. From the time of Charles I the Navy's fighting ships were specially built for the purpose; they were warships and nothing else, and their crews were specially trained, although the commanding officers, especially those of high rank, were often cavalrymen.

It was in the reign of Charles II that the real organization of the Royal Navy began, and it was a Londoner, Mr. Samuel Pepys, who was chiefly responsible. Pepys was just an ordinary Londoner, born in Salisbury Court, near St. Bride's Church in Fleet Street. His father was a tailor and the boy was educated at St. Paul's School, then in the cathedral churchyard. At the Restoration he became Secretary to the Navy Board and for the next thirty years he worked hard to make the Navy a real fighting service. When he became Clerk, in 1660, there were some good ships, but the Navy as a whole was badly organized and badly governed ; there was no proper system of training or promotion for the officers, the seamen were picked up in the ports as they were wanted, and the ships were laid up when there was no war. There was no organization in the dockyards, so that it took a long time to get a fleet ready for sea, and there was no organization at the Navy Office either.

Pepys, by hard work and attention to duty, altered all this, and before Charles II died he had given to England a fleet of thirty new battleships with all their attendant light craft. He had set up a completely new naval organization at the Admiralty; he had secured decent pay and service conditions for the seamen; he had drawn up a scheme of training and promotion for the officers, so that the ships were always ready for sea and there were always trained officers ready for them. It was Mr. Pepys who had forged the weapon that was to be used so effectively a century later by such great commanders as Rodney and Howe, St. Vincent and Nelson. Britain owes her command of the sea, and therefore her existence as an independent country, to the gift for leadership shown by a citizen of London.

All this time too, London had its own navy ; for the ships of the East India Company were armed as a protection against pirates, and in the next century the company kept a regular fleet of warships in Indian waters. These, too, were largely officered and manned by London men. From 1656, when the first " London " was launched, right down to our own day, there has always been a " London " in the Navy. London to-day still has its own navy whose headquarters are in H.M.S. " President " at Blackfriars.

What is true of the Navy is true also of the Army. The Londoner makes a fine soldier, noted for his resourcefulness, his contempt for danger, his steadiness under fire, his fine courage when things are going wrong, his dash in attack, and above all his unfailing humour.

The Cockney soldier always has his joke no matter how bad things may be.

The story of the Londoner under arms begins with the Danish invasions. Again and again the Danes attacked the city, sometimes winning a partial success, but always the Londoners returned to the attack and at the end London remained unconquered. At the battle of Hastings, too, the Londoners held the place of honour in the centre of the line as guardians of Harold's flag; and when the fight was over and the rest of the English army dead or scattered, the London men drew off in good order, carrying their wounded leader with them. They made their way back through the forest of the Weald, and so strong was their city that William dared not attack it directly, but passed along up the river to cross at Abingdon and sever the road to the Midlands. The Londoners had decided to resist, but when they saw that the Midland Earls would not help, they came to terms with William, electing him King of the English but keeping their independence. London was never conquered.

Right through the Middle Ages London kept its own army and saw fighting in all the wars. The men specially distinguished themselves at Crécy, where one whole division came from London. "The Londoners," says Sir John Froissart, who was present at the battle, "were noted for their bravery and for their skill with the longbow; the greater the odds against them the higher their courage rose and the more determined they became." Officers who saw the London men in battle in both the recent World Wars have said exactly the same things about them, only their skill is now with the rifle. It is interesting to note that it may have been the Londoners who first introduced gunpowder into European warfare, for in the year before the battle of Crécy the city bought powder, shot and something they call "gonnes", and Froissart tells us that the English used "gonnes" at Crécy for the first time.

H.M.S. "LONDON"

London troops fought in the Wars of the Roses and as volunteers in the wars of the Netherlands during the sixteenth century, but it was in the Civil War that they really proved themselves. London was the real leader in the struggle against Charles I, and it was the steadiness of the London infantry of the train-bands that prevented Edgehill from being a disastrous rout and kept off the Royalists at Brentford. Even after the New Model was formed the London regiments were the backbone of the infantry, and they were constantly being called upon to relieve besieged cities in the west of England, and to capture Royalist strongholds after Charles had been beaten in the field. London's own regiments, the Honourable Artillery Company and the City of London Regiment, were famous during the wars with Napoleon, and in our own time the London Rifles and the various Territorial regiments recruited within the London area have made themselves as famous as were their ancestors. London is still a leader in war.

But London is a leader in many other ways, and it is very largely owing to her leadership that Britain and the Empire have become great. Let us see how the citizens have decided some of the other important events in British history. We have already seen how they determined the course of the Norman Conquest. When William Rufus was killed and the Witan at Winchester was discussing whether his younger brother Henry should succeed, they asked the opinion of the Londoners and it was this that settled the issue. After the wars of Stephen it was the Londoners who decided that Henry of Anjou should become king ; they gave the crown to John on the death of Richard Lionheart ; they supported the barons against John and made Henry III king ; they helped Simon de Montfort, and they secured the succession of Edward I. By now it was generally recognized that the Londoners had the right to decide in a disputed succession and they exercised this right again and again, choosing Edward III on the deposition of his father,

and securing the throne to Richard II against the opposition of his uncles.   During the Wars of the Roses it was
their support that turned the scale.   Henry VII won his
crown at Bosworth, but it was the Londoners who made
him secure on the throne ;   and from then on, right
down to the days of George III, it was the Londoners
who really decided who should be king.

It is largely to London that we owe the British Empire.
Even before we had any overseas colonies the London
merchants were sending out expeditions to discover new
lands and to open up new sources of trade.   Martin
Frobisher, John Davis, and many another famous
explorer of Tudor times was employed by the merchants
of London and sailed in London ships manned by London
men, and when it came to making overseas settlements
London was again the leader.   The first attempt at
starting an overseas Empire was made in Northern
Ireland in the reign of James I.   Ulster had been
depopulated by rebellion and war ;   King James wanted
to resettle it with Scots from Galloway, and so he asked
the Londoners to provide the money.   After a lot of
discussion it was agreed to let James have a loan on
condition that London had a share in the settlement.
The City Corporation and the livery companies provided
the money, estates were granted for settlement, and a
body of citizens, called the Irish Society, was formed to
manage the project.   This Society still exists and is still
interested in the affairs of Ulster.   The town of Derry
(renamed Londonderry) was given to the Society, together
with the district of Coleraine, and both these were
settled by Londoners.

About the same time Londoners were becoming interested in North America.   Sir Walter Raleigh, who
may almost be considered a Londoner by adoption, if
not by birth, had suggested a settlement on the shores
of Chesapeake Bay as a base for attacks on the Spanish
treasure fleets, but the scheme had failed.   Now the
Londoners were taking up the idea again, this time

proposing a regular plantation on the lines of the Ulster settlement; and a company was formed, with a charter something like that of the old Merchant Adventurers. This London company then obtained from the King permission to plant settlements along the coast of North America. Having got this permission it formed other companies, the Virginia Company, the Massachusetts Bay Company and others, to manage the actual settlements. The first attempt was made in Raleigh's old Virginia colony and three ships were sent out from London on January 1st, 1607. They reached their destination some three months later, and set their passengers and stores ashore at a place which they named Jamestown. But the settlers were the wrong sort, mostly troublesome young people who had been shipped off by their relatives because they were a nuisance at home; their one idea was to get hold of Spanish gold as quickly as possible and return home to spend it. They quarrelled with their governor, they got into trouble with the Indians; and their settlement would soon have disappeared but for Captain John Smith, an adventurer who had served in most of the wars of Europe. Smith took charge, threatened to shoot any who disobeyed orders, and then, with the support of the better sort of settler, he set everybody to work clearing ground for crops and setting up defences. He saved the settlement. More settlers arrived and the present State of Virginia was founded. But even then the new Colony was not popular; people did not want to live overseas and some queer expedients were tried for getting settlers when the ships were ready to sail. On several such occasions the watch was ordered to round up all young people found on the streets after sunset. These were brought before the alderman next morning; the younger ones were whipped and handed over to their parents, but the older ones who were not apprentices were sentenced to transportation to Virginia. They were handed over to the Company, who agreed to carry them across to the colony, apprentice them there, and set them up with farms and wives when they had finished their time. The New England colonies farther north were settled in much the same way, but the settlers were mostly small farmers from the country round London and artisans from the little towns in the Home Counties. Many of them were Puritans who went because they wanted to worship in their own way, but it was chiefly the difficulty of getting a living at home that sent them out to America. Most of the money for the new settlements was provided by merchants in the city of London, and the management of the companies of adventurers to whom the charters were granted was in the hands of London citizens like Sir Richard Rich, Humphrey Weld a Lord Mayor, and John Pym, a Somerset man who had become a Londoner by coming to live in the city. These men saw in the new colonies not only a place to which the unemployed could be sent, but a source for the supply of corn, timber and other naval stores, and a nursery for seamen for the fleets.

The connection between the city and the colonies remained very close for over a century, and its strength was seen when the American War of Independence broke out. The city was entirely on the side of the colonies and took active steps to help them. Resolutions were passed by the Common Council expressing sympathy with the colonies in their struggle for freedom and the citizens of London did all they could to get the war stopped and an honourable agreement made. Had they been successful it is probable that the whole of North America would now be a part of the British Commonwealth.

When they saw that the King and his ministers were determined to force the colonies to give way, the Londoners took an active part in the war. They ordered that no London men should be allowed to join the regiments that were being raised for service in America; they sent the King's recruiting officers to prison for trying to enlist men in the city, and they refused to lend money to the Government for the prosecution of the war. They even passed resolutions of sympathy with the colonists in their fight for freedom, and they sent them money. Had not London helped in this way the colonies would probably have been beaten in the early days of the war, before they had learned to combine.

In the great fight for political freedom London was again the leader. Right back in the days of King John the Londoners had made a stand against arbitrary government, and it was only by their help that the barons had been able to compel John to agree to the Great Charter. The Charter itself is almost a London document for its clauses were settled in long discussions between the barons and the leading citizens, and before it was presented to the King it was read out to a great meeting of citizens held in the cathedral and agreed to by them. Right through the Middle Ages London had been on the side of liberty, and step by step her support had helped to build up the powers of the Parliament, a body whose constitution is very like that of London's own government.

During the Middle Ages London had worked with the barons to check the power of the King. After the Wars of the Roses, when it looked as though the barons were becoming too powerful, London helped the King to check the power of the great nobles, with the result that in Tudor times the nobles were replaced by the King's Ministers of State. When, under the Stuarts, this form of government threatened the liberties of the people, London again led the opposition. It was a London merchant named Chambers who took a stand against the arbitrary collection of Ship Money a year before John Hampden, who was also a London citizen, refused to pay. When Charles I, eleven years later, ordered the arrest of the Five Members, it was in the city that they found safety. London too had been the leader of the opposition to Laud's proposals for setting

THE FIRE OF LONDON, 1940

221

up an autocratic Church and against the Earl of Strafford's policy of a strong central government. We have already read how the Londoners fought in the Great Civil War, how they secured the recall of the King when it seemed that the Army was going to set up a military tyranny, and how they turned against James II and forced him from the country when he too tried to be an absolute monarch. Later, in the reign of George III, when it seemed as though the Cabinet and Parliament would free themselves from popular control, it was the city once more that took the lead against them.

Both Government and Parliament are to-day controlled by public opinion, and it is to the city that we owe this. Public opinion is very largely expressed through the Press which is free to publish the speeches of Ministers and Members of Parliament, even when they are made in the House. In this way their opinions and actions are made known to the public and are commented on in leading articles and by letters which people write to the editors of the papers. The freedom of the Press was won by the city during the long struggle between Mr. Wilkes, the Editor of the *North Briton*, and Parliament in the reign of George III. This struggle is mixed up with the American War of Independence and, as you will find it described in your history books, I will only mention it here. Meetings were held in the city; the Common Council passed resolutions in favour of free elections and a free press, and at one point in the struggle King George was told by the Lord Mayor that if there were any traitors in the country they were His Majesty himself and his Ministers. The fight for freedom was won, but the price we had to pay for it was the loss of the American Colonies.

When the French Revolution broke out it was feared that it might spread to this country, as it very probably would have done had not the city won its fight for freedom of speech and writing. Had it done so there might very well have been scenes enacted here such as were being seen in Paris, for there was great distress here and the mob was as large and as dangerous as that of Paris. In 1794 the harvest failed and there was a danger of famine. It was famine in Paris that had made the Revolution a success, but in London the city authorities handled the situation firmly and wisely. Actual rioting was firmly dealt with by the citizens. The Artillery Company was called to arms and a volunteer defence force raised; the leaders of riots were arrested, tried before the Lord Mayor and sent to prison. But steps were taken to relieve distress by the introduction of food rationing, by releasing the city's supplies of corn which were held for just such an emergency, and by raising a fund for the relief of the destitute. These measures were successful and the danger passed. There was some rioting, but it was easily stopped.

In the long struggle against Napoleon, London again took the lead. When war threatened, the city voted bounties to encourage enlistment, funds were raised to supply comforts for the men of the Expeditionary Force that was sent to Flanders, and a volunteer Home Guard was enlisted in London, an example that was quickly followed by the rest of the country. The war went badly ; the British were driven out of Flanders and, when the harvest failed, trade almost stopped and even the munition factories began to close down; many people began to say that we ought to get out of a war which did not concern us. But London stood firm, and when Napoleon gathered an army for the invasion of England the city once again took the lead. Everyone knew that the attack would be made against London, because, if the city were taken, then Britain would be conquered, and so every effort was made for its defence. Ten regiments of " Home Guards " were formed in addition to the regular city forces of the Artillery Company and the London Fusiliers, whilst all the rivermen were formed into a Naval Brigade for the defence of the river. Like our modern Home Guard these men were never called upon to fight, but their mere presence made Napoleon delay in order to strengthen his forces and, like Hitler in 1940, he lost his chance. The Navy kept the seas, Nelson defeated the French fleet at Trafalgar and Napoleon decided to deal with Russia first. He wasted his strength there and, whilst he was doing this, Britain was able to raise an army to invade Spain, where a popular rising made success possible. Throughout the whole of the war London kept the resistance spirit alive. The citizens raised loans for arming the resistance movements in Europe; they demanded inquiries when things went wrong; they rewarded successful generals and they encouraged the peoples of Europe to continue the fight. London saved Europe by the courage, the endurance and the public spirit of her people.

After the Napoleonic Wars the great task before the country was reconstruction, a task which took nearly half a century to complete and, in this too, London took the lead. The wealth of the country was enormously increased by the introduction of machinery and the setting up of new industries. These were mainly in the North and the Midlands, but their development was made possible by the money that had been accumulated by the city. It was with this money that the new factories were built; without it, and the world-wide financial and commercial experience of London, the new industries could never have been developed. The city was still powerful, but it was becoming lost in a new and greater London which was without unity; it was just a collection of villages and small towns connected by buildings but separated by each having its own government. The country as a whole was in much the same condition. The old unity of squires and farmers which had been England was broken up and a new England was forming, an England which, like the new London, was without unity. The first step towards building a new unity in the country was to get the industrial classes represented in Parliament, and it was for this purpose that the agitation for the Reform Bill was started. In this agitation the City Corporation took a leading part. Resolutions against the Corn Laws were passed when these were being proposed, and when they became law in 1815, the city continued its protests until the laws were repealed thirty years later; petitions were sent to Parliament protesting against the treatment of the poor and declaring that their distress was caused mainly by the policy of the Government; and resolutions were passed in favour of the Reform Bills. After the Reform Act was passed the city continued to agitate, this time for the reform of the municipal corporations. London not only agitated, she set the example. The City Corporation reformed itself along lines that were afterwards followed by Parliament when it set up new forms of local government, especially for the new manufacturing towns of the North and the Midlands.

During the last hundred years the chief matters of interest have been the growth of commerce and the development of the interior of Africa and of the islands of the Pacific Ocean. Here again London has led. The example of London in fostering the settlement and growth of our first colonial empire in the seventeenth century was followed in that of the second during the nineteenth. Australia, New Zealand, South Africa and Canada were developed with money supplied by the city banking houses, and by means of companies whose headquarters were in the city. Much of the early growth of the United States of America and of the Republics of South America was paid for in the same way. Through the century, too, London took the lead in securing liberty to oppressed peoples. The movement for Greek independence was greatly strengthened by the attitude of the city, and patriots like Garibaldi of Italy were always sure of a welcome and of support in London. Here they were able to express their views freely, and, so long as they did nothing that was likely to cause a riot, they could even form societies, hold meetings, and run newspapers. At one time or another practically every one of the leaders of reform, or even of revolutionary movements in Europe, has found a refuge and a welcome in London. Distress caused by earthquake, fire, famine or other calamity in any part of the world has always been met by the creation of a Lord Mayor's Fund into which subscriptions flow from all parts of the world because people of all nationalities know that any cause supported by London will be a worthy one, and that any fund administered by the Lord Mayor of London will be used wisely and to the best advantage of those in distress.

London has produced many leaders, too, in science, in the arts and in literature. It would take a whole book to describe the achievements of great Londoners in these spheres; a mere list of names would fill several pages. No city in the whole world has ever produced a longer list of great writers, painters or scientists and thinkers, and nowhere can art, science or literature be studied better than in London, with its great schools, its museums, its libraries and its art galleries, its theatres and concert halls.

In earlier days London's opinions and leadership were generally expressed by the action of the City Corporation, but now the expression of opinion comes largely through the Press, and we have already seen something of the way in which it works. To-day, too, this expression of opinion is made through great public meetings or by the foundation of societies for the support of some cause, and in many cases the success of these depends on the support they receive in London. We are the citizens of no mean city, and, if we love our London as we should, we shall do everything we can to see that, in our day, she is worthy of her great past.

Published by Evans Brothers Ltd.,
Montague House, Russell Square, London,
and printed in Great Britain by
Butler & Tanner Ltd., Frome and London